HEALTHY HOME

HEALTHY

JILL BLAKE

HOME

*A practical and resourceful
guide to making your own home
fit for body, mind, and spirit*

KEY PORTER BOOKS

Published in Canada in 1998 by

Key Porter Books Ltd.

Canadian Cataloguing in Publication Data

Blake, Jill
                    healthy home
Includes index.

ISBN 1-55013-973-8

1. Interior decoration. 2. Interior decoration – Physchological aspects. I. Title.

NK2113.B64 1998   747   C98-930573-2

Key Porter Books Limited

70 The Esplanade

Toronto, Ontario

Canada M5E 1R2

www.keyporter.com

This book was conceived, designed, and produced by
THE IVY PRESS LIMITED

Art director: Terry Jeavons
Designer: Alan Osbahr
Commissioning Editor: Viv Croot
Edited by: Ann Kramer
Page layout: Alan Osbahr and Siân Keogh
Picture research: Arlene Bridgewater
Three-dimensional models: David Donkin, Mark Jamieson
Illustrations: Jerry Fowler, Lorraine Harrison
Feng Shui Consultant: Jane Butler-Biggs

Printed in Hong Kong

98 99 00 01 6 5 4 3 2 1

CONTENTS

6   PREFACE

PART ONE
22   CREATING A HARMONIOUS HOME

24   SPACE AND HARMONY
Organizing space for healthy living

56   LIGHT
Bringing natural light and artificial light into the home

76   COLOR
Using color for health, harmony, and style

112   SCENTS AND SOUND
Enhancing your home with scents and sound

132   LIVING THINGS
The health-giving value of plants and living things

PART TWO
156   CREATING AN ECO-FRIENDLY HOME

158   HEALING A HOME

160   A Healthier Home

170   A Resource-Friendly Hoɪ

182   Glossary

184   Useful Addresses

188   Index

192   Acknowledgments

I have always believed homes should be planned for happy living and that, because no two families have an identical lifestyle, requirements, or the same budget, every home will be a highly individual unit, planned, designed, and decorated to suit those who are going to live in it. This drive to individuality can be seen clearly in a street of houses, all built to the same design. As soon as new owners move into one of the houses, it takes on an entirely different look from the house next door, both inside and out, as the new owners plan rooms, choose color schemes, select furniture and furnishings, and plant the yard to suit themselves. "Nest-building" is the current buzzword used to describe this phenomenon—I prefer to call it creative homemaking.

For at least a hundred years, there has been plenty of help and advice available for would-be homemakers from the publication of august tomes on household management through to the more recent proliferation of specialized and general magazines and supplements, to say nothing of television programs all devoted to different aspects of interior design, decoration, furnishings, and garden planning.

Today there is much more to the art, science, and craft of homemaking than in previous decades.

PREFACE

We want our homes to be attractive and possibly stylish, as well as being happy places. We also want them to be healthy. We are aware of the problems of pollutants that can enter our homes either from the materials used to build and furnish our homes, or that can creep in from outside. We want to make our homes more environmentally friendly, to run them without making a drain on energy and other resources, and without using materials that will damage our wider environment. The current interest in the ancient philosophy of feng shui also reflects our concern to create a healthy and harmonious home environment.

Interest in alternative energy, practical insulation, recycling, and organic gardening is widespread and has already affected governments, builders, developers, architects, manufacturers, and retailers, as well as homemakers. Fortunately, therefore, we are in a good position to use environmentally friendly products for the home.

But health is not only about being environmentally aware; it is also about creating a healthy atmosphere. In this book I have tried to help you create a healthier home by suggesting ways of planning, designing, decorating, and furnishing, as well as fitting everything into the available space, that will suit your particular lifestyle and which will be sympathetic not only to the environment, but also to the original architectural style of your home. I have also recommended user-friendly materials, healthy housekeeping, maintenance, and cleaning, as well as giving some advice on how to heal existing problems.

While researching this book, I have gained an even greater respect for the way our grandmothers and great-grandmothers ran their homes efficiently and economically with very little in the way of appliances. Many of the things they did were not only practical but also thrifty—and healthy; they certainly knew about recycling, and we could take a leaf from their books.

I hope you will enjoy reading *Healthy Home* and that it will help you create as healthy and happy an environment as possible, in which you and your family can live with pleasure, where you can shut the door on the outside world, relax, be stimulated, follow various hobbies and pursuits, and, above all, improve the quality of your life.

Jill Blake

JILL BLAKE

BEGINNINGS

The function of a home is to provide shelter, but approaches and styles have varied through time and place, often moving interior and exterior design well beyond basic needs. This elegant street in London, for instance, reflected the wealth of its original occupants.

Toward the end of the 19th century, the Art Nouveau movement rejected the harshness of industrialism in favor of natural materials and craft-based furniture and furnishings. Flowing lines reflected forms found in nature.

WHERE DID IT ALL BEGIN: the enthusiasm for design, decoration, color, and style expressed in the desire we all have to create our own special environment?

Initially homes provided a basic shelter from the elements, although maybe even then there were attempts to stamp the inhabitant's personality onto the fabric. But, by and large, it was only the rich and aristocratic who were able to have their houses and castles architecturally designed and the interiors styled to personal taste, including carpets and furniture. In fact, in some cases, the designer even provided an accurate plan stipulating the exact positioning of furniture and artifacts, all of which had to be replaced exactly by household staff after accommodating guests, or cleaning. Homes such as these were designed to impress royalty or nobility; they were rarely comfortable or homey!

Beginning in the 18th century, the Industrial Revolution brought

enormous changes in Europe, not least in the ways buildings and their contents were constructed. The then emerging middle classes, with new-found wealth, made a cult of the home and began to build smaller and often spectacular houses. The Nash Terraces in London and the flamboyant Royal Pavilion in Brighton paved the way for an increasing interest in design and architecture, so that an elegantly designed house, both inside and out, became the aspiration of all but the most impoverished.

But interior design, as we understand it today, did not really come into fashion until the inter-war period, when contemporary decorators such as Elsie de Wolfe, Sybil Colefax, Syrie Maugham, and Eileen Gray became fashionable, and the rich and famous commissioned them to design the interiors of their houses.

At much the same time there was a vogue for Modernism, or the International style, which was based on functional, minimalist design, advocated by architects such as Walter Gropius, who founded the Bauhaus school in 1919, Mies van der Rohe, Le Corbusier, and Marcel Breur, who believed in applying the principles of industrial design to the interior—rejecting the past completely. Interestingly, this approach and style is now re-emerging with the increasing popularity of lofts—large open-plan interiors that are often constructed in old warehouses or factories.

Interior design and decoration—and of course building—was

Modernism embraced industrial processes and moved design away from the natural environment to a starkness that is evident in the extreme minimalism shown here.

put under wraps during World War II, and for some time after. Shortages of materials meant that it was only possible to build fairly simple or functional houses. Now this has changed dramatically—in Britain, for example, change began with the 1951 Festival of Britain, which claimed to promote the best of British design—and interior design has become a fashion industry, with new trends appearing and disappearing almost as fast as in the clothing industry.

ECO-DESIGN These days

much is written, discussed, and televised on the need to design and build "green" homes. This began during the 1960s and 1970s with the greater awareness of the need to conserve energy. Alternative energy centers, such as the Centre for Alternative Technology in Machynlleth in Wales, appeared, and show houses were displayed at exhibitions or built on demonstration sites.

Initially the main concerns were conservation—of energy, water, and other resources—and the use of sustainable building materials. But although many of us may not yet have gotten around to the most basic energy conservation in our own homes, the industry has moved on from this stage, and there is now a growing movement among architects, industrial and

interior designers, garden designers, and even builders and manufacturers to consider the wider ecological aspects of the buildings they create and the materials and products they use.

True ecological design looks at the home and other buildings in relation to the wider environment. Ecological design is concerned with saving or replanting trees and other native plants; preserving streams, lakes, wetlands, and local landscape, perhaps building sympathetically around them; and reducing pollution in the construction process. The height and width of buildings, too, are planned so they are not starkly aggressive or dwarf the landscape, perhaps screened with existing trees, rocks, hillsides, or other natural features, or with the landscape redesigned around them.

Ecological designers have also reassessed vernacular design, using color, form, materials, and structural

Recent years have seen an increasingly strong movement towards ecologically influenced design that emphasizes the need for homes to harmonize with the natural environment both in style and materials.

traditions that are native to the particular area, often using local brick, stone, and clay and even indigenous soil. This way, they create a building that is truly at home in its environment. As a result of this trend, many traditional and natural building products have been reintroduced, such as wood frames, clay blocks, lime mortar, and plaster, many of which may be recycled. Even earth and grass are used as building materials, and some of the buildings themselves may be partly buried in the landscape.

This approach to building design is becoming increasingly important, and there are various associations and organizations that you can contact if you are planning to build or convert to a more environmentally friendly home. Recently, too, in Germany and Scandinavia, a movement has emerged devoted to "building biology," or *Baubiologie,* which combines the scientific and ecological approach with a holistic view of the relationship between buildings and people, so that buildings are also seen as living organisms.

DEFINING
A HEALTHY
HOME

As daily life becomes increasingly pressurized, there is unprecedented interest in nest-building, creating homes that satisfy deep needs. But despite pressure from television and magazine features, creating a healthy home need not be expensive.

TODAY, we can barely pick up a magazine, switch on the television, or browse through a bookstore without realizing that tremendous pressure is being put on all of us to create the "perfect" environment, one that expresses our personality and at the same time is stylish, stunning, environmentally friendly—and effortless. And many of these magazine and television features suggest that it is both inexpensive and very easy to carry out an effective "makeover," whether of just one room, your entire house, or your yard.

Of course, what you don't actually see is the army of helpers who carry out the decorating, produce those stunning furnishings, re-upholster the furniture, lay spectacular floorings, hang pictures, and position tasteful accessories such as lamps or wall hangings. Nor is the cost ever mentioned. What you are most likely to see are so-called interior designers discussing the current trends and trying to impose their taste and will on the viewer and the reader—and in doing so often promoting the latest, and quite possibly short-lived, styles and ideas.

But creating a healthy and happy home is not just about following design trends unthinkingly. It is also about meeting personal needs, about creating the right space for you. Professional interior designers will not impose their will on their clients; they will be at great pains to ferret out the needs, requirements, likes, and dislikes of all of those who will be living in the house.

So what constitutes a healthy, happy, and harmonious home—apart from one that is light and spacious, welcoming, practically planned, attractively decorated and furnished, filled with natural and user-friendly materials, and surrounded by a verdant garden?

A really happy and healthy home has an indefinable quality; you can sense good "vibes" the moment you enter the front door, sometimes even as you walk up the front path. This instinctive reaction cannot be explained by builders, property developers, realtors, or "house doctors," a growing band of people who ferret out the history of your house or advise on improving it to make it more saleable. It is a hard feeling to pin down, but it is certainly one that we need, so much so that many would-be purchasers today

call on feng shui consultants to advise on the most favorable aspects of a property and whether it will be good for the health and luck of the occupants.

A truly healthy home is a place that is good for you and your family not only physically but also mentally, emotionally, and spiritually. It should be somewhere pleasurable to return to in the evening, somewhere where you can relax, shrug off the worries and tensions of the day, and be yourself, a place that contains some personal space where you can shut the door occasionally on the rest of the world. It should be a creative environment, where you can indulge in cooking, gardening, sewing, and other hobbies, and somewhere that is comfortable enough for you to flop down and watch television, listen to music,

read a book, play a musical instrument, pursue a craft, in short to do whatever it is that you want to do without feelings of tension or anxiety.

Your home should also have an invigorating ambience; it should be a pleasure to wake in the morning in surroundings that you have created yourself, perhaps surrounded by a color that suggests bright, warm sunshine even on the coldest, bleakest, and grayest of days. Your home environment should inspire, stimulate, and calm, and, above all, be a source of great enjoyment both to yourself and others who enter it.

Finally, a healthy home should be nonpolluting, both for your health and that of the wider environment. It should be safe, free from toxins, and as full as possible of natural and user-friendly materials.

A healthy home has an almost indefinable quality— it just feels right. More tangibly, it should be light, airy, comfortable, welcoming, and non-polluting. Above all, your home should be a place that enhances your physical and mental well-being.

TAKING STOCK

Don't rush into changing your home. The first step toward creating a healthy home is to get a feel of the space you live in. Change nothing for a year or, if you prefer, paint everything white so you can observe how changing light and seasons affect your home.

BEGINNINGS ARE always difficult, and creating a healthy home takes time; it can't be done overnight, no matter how easy a televised makeover appears. Most of us won't be working with professional designers; we will be doing our own design and decoration, and in the profusion of advice we will be offered, it is often hard to know where to start and what to choose.

Possibly the very best advice is to start by doing nothing, except spending time getting a feel for and understanding of your surroundings. This is not always easy, especially if you have lived in your property for some time. Try to forget all the existing color schemes, decorations, and furnishings and imagine that you have a clean slate. Try to remember how you felt when you first saw the inside of your home; if you can't remember, get a friend or family member to jog your memory.

And if you have just moved, or are about to, don't rush to change anything. Until you have lived in your home for at least a year, experiencing each of the changing seasons, you will not know how your various rooms feel in spring, summer, fall, or winter and how the natural light affects them as the seasons pass. If you really can't live

> **"Have nothing in your house which you know not to be useful—or believe to be beautiful"** (WILLIAM MORRIS)

Traditional Shaker homes made good and thrifty use of materials at hand. Their approach to homemaking was practical. For example, they created space by hanging chairs on walls.

with the existing decor, just paint everything white or some other fairly neutral color; live with bare floorboards and simple blinds at the windows while you get an awareness of how you want your home to be.

Apply this same rule to patios, sunrooms, and gardens. Wait to see what is already present and what growing things will emerge during the spring and summer and how their arrival changes light and shade inside the home and out.

BEAUTY AND FUNCTION

Once you have a feel for your home, you can then get to work. Really successful design is about the fusion of the practical with the aesthetic—surfaces, materials, furniture, and all the components of an interior should be chosen to suit the purpose and function of the area in which they will be used as well as reflecting the particular lifestyle of those who will be living there. And it is these considerations that will dictate the choice and color of rooms, the texture and wearability of fabrics, and how all surfaces are treated. And, of course, consideration must be paid to the original architectural style in which the building was constructed.

Good design and the resulting functional, comfortable, and healthy homes are the result of careful planning and working out of one grand master plan. To achieve a good and sympathetic environment, you need to plan your home and the spaces within carefully, and the first section of this book gives you detailed advice that will be helpful.

But you need more than clever, functional planning: you also need to think about budget and how much money you have available. Creating a healthy home need not be expensive; you will probably have to work with existing structural constraints and may find that you can incorporate many existing items. Words such as salvage, recycling, and thrift can take on whole new meanings as you make use of what already exists to create your healthy home. In fact, many things now associated with crafting tradition began as the practical use of materials which were on hand. The patchwork quilt, for instance, was a way of using scraps of fabric, and this craft has now become an art form. In Shaker communities, old metal was used to create lamps and boxes.

USING FENG SHUI

MANY PEOPLE TODAY ARE increasingly interested in using feng shui to achieve a healthy and harmonious home. Put simply, feng shui is an ancient art of placement, based on the idea that the way you organize your home, choose rooms, decorate them, and place your furniture can enhance well-being. Some of the principles are different from those of conventional interior design, but there are also many parallels.

Feng shui is not new, although it has only recently arrived in the West. It is an ancient Chinese philosophy, with origins that date back at least 5,000 years. Translated literally, feng shui means "wind and water" and its main aim is to achieve balance and harmony with the natural environment by arranging or altering your surroundings according to certain principles. Applied to the home, or to offices and other buildings, feng shui can be used to enhance the happiness, prosperity, and good fortune of the occupants, while creating serene, healthy, and balanced surroundings.

FORM AND COMPASS

There are many different schools of feng shui, some of which have been adapted for modern use. The oldest is the Form school, which places emphasis on the importance of natural landscapes—hills, mountains, rivers, and other landforms—for enhancing well-being and evaluating the quality of a location. Gradually this evolved into the Compass school, which introduced the idea that specific points of the compass exert

unique influences on different aspects of life. The south, for instance, with its orientation toward the sun's heat, has a more energizing effect than the colder north. Today, feng shui practitioners use blends of the different schools according to needs or circumstances as they arise.

CHI

Feng shui is based on the belief that there is an invisible life force or energy known as chi that circulates both within ourselves and throughout the universe. In order to live well and healthily, we need to harness this force and encourage a healthy flow of chi energy into our homes and lives. Feng shui practitioners would argue that if our lives are stagnant or if we are depressed or lacking

in energy, it is because this fundamental chi energy has itself become blocked, negative, or unhealthy, sometimes because the spaces within our homes are cluttered, poorly organized, or destructive in some way.

A key concept in feng shui is that everything in the universe is made up of two opposing but complementary energies—yin and yang. Yin, for instance, is dark; yang is light. Health and well-being come when our homes reflect a balance between the two.

FIVE ELEMENTS

Another important concept is that of the five elements or energies: fire, metal, wood, water, and earth. According to feng shui, these are the basic elements

Good feng shui aims to balance yin and yang. The green plants, harmonizing colors, and the play of light and shade in this area (left) produce a healthy balance, although the sharp corners could disrupt energy. Clear spaces and use of curves in the kitchen (right) promote the smooth flow of chi; red flowers boost fire energy.

YIN	YANG
Shade	Light
Female	Male
Passive	Active
Moon	Sun
Earth	Sky
Soft	Firm
Water	Fire
Winter	Summer
Cold	Heat

of the universe, and each of us is born into one of them. Together they create an unending cycle that can be either creative or destructive. Each of the elements is also associated with a particular compass direction, color, and various other attributes, so by introducing one or more of the elements into your home, you can boost, enhance, or activate one of the energies according to your personal needs, thus improving your life situation.

Professional feng shui practitioners spend many years perfecting their art, and some of the principles behind feng shui are quite complex. But feng shui is also all about encouraging us to return to a more intuitive approach to placement, so if you find that your home feels good and if you feel well in it,

then you have probably, though unwittingly, followed good feng shui practice.

Much of feng shui practice, like sensible interior design, is based on common sense. A room that is uncluttered, for instance, obviously has an ambience that encourages uncluttered thought. We can do very little about where our homes are located, but we can do a great deal about how we organize our living spaces inside our homes, and feng shui principles can be incorporated quite simply by changing the use of a room, rearranging furniture, using certain colors, balancing light and shade, or simply by adding plants, mirrors, or other objects to boost or activate healthy energy flows into and through the living spaces of the home.

What a feng shui consultant does

Just as some people call in professional interior designers, so too it is possible to call in a professional feng shui consultant.

A consultant will:

■ look at a property, ask details of your birth—place, date, and time—and draw up a horoscope to establish whether you and your new home will be compatible;

■ possibly check on previous occupants to establish how their health, wealth, and happiness progressed while they were living there and will advise on whether you are likely to enjoy the same prosperity, or bad luck. What suits one person may not, of course, be right for another.

■ produce a written or verbal report on the feng shui of the property, including details of the chi energy flowing in and around the building and whether or not you will prosper in your potential new surroundings

■ report on the changes you may need to make to improve the feng shui of the building. If these are fairly minimal, the consultant may recommend buying the property; if they are too difficult or costly or if the home is unsuitable for you, the consultant may suggest that you find an alternative

■ a feng shui consultant will also advise on your existing home and, if there are problems, will suggest simple remedies.

SETTING PRIORITIES

For relaxed living your home must match your lifestyle. This minimalist style with its white walls, natural wood floors, and varying levels is streamlined, beautifully designed, and easy to maintain. It would be good for adults, but unsuitable for children.

THERE ARE MANY STYLES that you can choose for your home. The building itself may influence your final choice, but ultimately style must also relate to and reflect your personal lifestyle. A streamlined, minimalist interior, totally devoid of clutter and with lots of light, wide, open spaces, and vast glazed windows, furnished with the bare essentials, may well suit a single person or childless couple. But this style is rarely compatible with toddlers and small children, and may well be unsafe for them. So the arrival of children may mean moving into a more conventional living space or making structural changes. Flexibility has to be an essential ingredient when styling and planning your home.

Age and life stage will effect your choices. If you are in your 20s or 30s, and lead a busy life, you may prefer a fairly streamlined minimalist interior, which is easy to clean and maintain, and perhaps no yard to tend. If children arrive, you may want to change properties and add a yard. If you are in your middle years, with an active family, you may prefer a cozier lifestyle, and may need a two- or even four-bedroom house with more than one bathroom, a living and dining room, surrounded by a good-sized yard with the potential for creating several different outdoor spaces—somewhere for children to play, somewhere to enjoy *al fresco* meals, and perhaps to plant a vegetable and fruit garden. As more changes occur, you may even consider changing the use of various rooms in the house according to changing needs.

You may either choose to move several times to accommodate life changes, or to adapt the same property in many different ways over the years. Moving can be highly stressful and, like planning a house, needs to be planned as carefully as possible in order for such a big change to run smoothly.

THE NEED FOR PLANNING
Whatever stage you have reached, you will want to be able to live comfortably in your home, so it needs to be well-planned with plenty of storage space to accommodate the clutter of family living. To achieve harmony, you

For most families the arrival of children alters the definition of a healthy home and changes priorities. In this home, small tables might need to be moved, but the hard-wearing surfaces and materials, level floors, and access to the yard or patio are all ideal.

will need to plan your space so you can move around and perform various tasks relatively effortlessly; you will also need different rooms for different activities: sitting, relaxing, sleeping, and cooking. Style will play a part in planning, but so, too, should comfort and efficiency.

USING COLOR

You can get a great deal of enjoyment from deciding on design, playing with patterns, and choosing color schemes. Color is an important part of any healthy home because the colors you select will play a major role in creating mood and ambience; they can stimulate or relax, provide warmth, or cool down a space. The type of patterns you use, your furniture, curtains, and blinds, will all help to create a distinctive style as well as an appropriate atmosphere in your home.

Color and style are discussed more fully later in the book, but when you are working with a whole house or apartment, don't forget the importance of whole-house color coordination.

If you live in a fairly small house or apartment, aim to carry color on from one room into another; this way the whole area will feel more spacious and create a sense of continuity. The hall, stairs, and landings in particular should be warm and welcoming, and should relate to all the areas or rooms leading off. You can use floor color to provide this link, either by having the same floor color throughout (it need not be all the same material or texture) or by using a patterned

Color sets atmosphere and mood. Vibrant yellow walls and a red carpet make a welcoming hallway. Moving the yellow up the stairs provides a link with the rest of the house and a feeling of continuity.

multicolored flooring in the hall and on the stairs and then separating out individual colors to use singly in different rooms.

Whole-house scheming does not mean that a whole home has to be decorated in similar colors; this could be extremely boring. But aim to work with a similar color palette: choose several colors for the main surface, but make changes from area to area, introducing some interestingly colored accessories, which are easy to change and which will help to define the function and style of the space. You can work mainly with neutrals, or with warm or cool colors, and bring in sharp contrast by using attractive accessories.

You can also use color to enhance good features in your home, play down less attractive ones, and improve the proportions of different rooms. Color can also lighten dark areas, warm cool spaces, and create feelings of intimacy or space.

LIGHT, SENSORY PLEASURE, AND NATURE

Planning a healthy home also means making the best use of light, both natural and artificial. Aim to let as much natural light into your home as possible, and then use artificial lighting to enhance dark areas, ensure safety, and provide well-lit working areas.

Making links with nature also brings harmony and health into the home. In order to make your home healthy and pleasant, aim to create indoor green spaces in your living areas, even more so if you have no yard. It is surprising what you can do with houseplants, herbs, and flowers; they brighten the home and improve the air quality. Outdoor green spaces, too, whether yard, patio, or balcony, provide pleasurable and relaxing additions to every home.

A healthy home should also be pleasing to the senses and calm. Scents, pleasant sounds, and water features enhance every environment; fabrics can muffle intrusive sounds and are also a pleasure to touch and live with. A quiet home, free from unwanted sounds, is conducive to health and constructive family life and allows for times of meditation during the day.

WORKING WITH NATURAL PRODUCTS

Whatever decisions you reach on planning, color, and furnishing, aim to use as many natural materials as possible. They are healthier and more pleasant and enjoyable to live with than synthetic fabrics and artificial materials; they are also likely to be more tactile.

A healthy home is nonpolluting. We know now that many products, such as lead-based paint and asbestos, which was once used in many homes as an insulator and fire barrier, are serious health hazards. But we are still using plastics and foam for upholstery, which are serious fire hazards and which give off dangerous fumes if they do catch fire. We also use laminates and composite board for built-in furniture and kitchen cabinets, and vinyl floor and wall coverings, all of which give off formaldehyde. Many homes also contain synthetic fabrics as well as dangerous adhesives and glues, and home decorators use highly caustic substances for stripping off old paint. All these should be replaced with more user-friendly products, even if this does mean there will be a little more work and elbow grease involved.

It is far better to furnish and decorate using natural materials: wood from fast-growing deciduous trees like pine or recycled lumber; fabrics such as linens, cotton, and wool; wood, cork, linoleum, or rubber for flooring; and recycled quarry tiles, flagstones, and earthenware squares instead of vinyl.

Furnish and decorate your home with natural materials: cane, wood, rushes, and organic paints. Avoid using synthetic materials and other harmful, toxic, or polluting substances such as formaldehyde or vinyl.

Introducing natural sounds and scents from the garden, living with the smell of cut flowers, and encouraging daylight into the house are very simple ways of enriching your home and making links with nature.

Book-filled shelves are practical but also create an interesting archway, while a polished wooden floor links the two areas. The result is a calm, peaceful, and ordered living space.

POINTS TO CONSIDER

Buying a home is one of the most stressful life decisions. Plan it carefully and make a list of your needs before deciding. An urban home gives access to shopping, transportation, and other services; a home in the country brings you closer to nature, but will create dependence on a car.

IF LIFE WERE PERFECT, we might well elect to design and build our own homes by employing an architect, builder, and interior designer to realize our ideas on an attractive plot of land with services such as electricity, natural gas, and drainage nearby. And of course it would need to be conveniently situated for work, schools, shopping, leisure activities, and socializing—difficult if not almost impossible to find in most areas of our overcrowded world.

If you are embarking on designing and building your own home, try to plan from the inside out. List all your requirements, but maintain a flexible approach. Think ahead and plan for what may be very different needs in five, ten, or even twenty years' time. This will mean planning the interior so that certain spaces are flexible and

multipurpose, and walls will be easy to move or alter. The practical Japanese system of sliding shoji is an interesting idea, although perhaps not one that many of us would use.

If you are starting from scratch, you will also be able to consider incorporating environmental and health aspects into your home by installing energy-saving devices such as solar heating, adequate insulation, double- or triple-glazing, and water recycling, asking your architect to build your home around your definitive list, subject to financial considerations.

Alternatively, you may opt for a form of prefabricated building, or either a modern or older barn or wood-framed building that can be moved from one site to another and adapted to suit your needs.

Most of us have to choose a property that is already built and has had previous occupants. You may choose a period property, or something more modern. Always think about your requirements before making a final decision.

You will first need to decide where you want to live: town, city, suburbia, or countryside. Rural sites are often considered ideal for bringing up young children or for retirement. But think carefully before making this decision. Shopping, schools, and medical services may be some distance away, and you will need to check out the efficiency of public transportation if you are concerned about the environmental implications of car ownership.

If you opt for a city or town location, check the proximity of parks and other green sites as well as local schools, shopping, and public transportation. In some cities, these can be as scarce as in the countryside. Also consider the problems of air and noise pollution. If you are buying an apartment, check access, including elevators and car parking. You may find that a home in a leafy suburb will provide you with a good compromise.

Once you have decided on location and the size and type of property, contact local realtors in the area of your choice and also read the advertisements in local newspapers. Be as precise and definitive with a realtor as you would be with an architect if you are building your own home; don't waste time making appointments to view unsuitable ones.

When you do go to view, keep an open mind. Don't be deterred by other peoples' decorations, furniture, furnishings, and carpets. Imagine the rooms as if they were empty and undecorated, a blank slate on which you will create your own home. Look carefully at the fabric and state of the structure and also check how much natural daylight the rooms receive. Think, too, about orientation—the way in which rooms face. Determine which rooms receive early morning sun, ideal for bathrooms and kitchens, and which receive the afternoon sun, good for living or dining rooms. It is important to consider which way the garden or patio faces: a north- or northeast-facing garden will be cold and dark in the afternoon. Also be aware of overshadowing buildings or tall

trees. Both will shade your property, and tree roots can also damage the foundations. If you are buying an apartment, you may also want to establish discreetly who your neighbors are.

But in the final analysis it is up to you to choose a home that has the right vibes, where you and your family will be happy, which will suit your needs, requirements, and lifestyle, and which has the potential to be designed and decorated to your personal tastes, whether it be a modern, functional loft space, or a traditional home.

FENG SHUI
SITES
If you are a devotee of feng shui, you may well decide to call in a feng shui consultant who will see whether the house is suitable for you and your family, examine its location and orientation, and look at whether there are adverse environmental factors such as pollution. Other points that he or she will consider will include the health and happiness of the current occupants.

In feng shui an ideal site should also mean the building is backed by a hill or mountain because beneficial chi will flow into the building, and detrimental chi will be deflected away. If this is not possible, tall trees or even high buildings could be substituted, but they should not be too close or they will cut natural light; tall buildings can also be oppressive and interfere with privacy. There should be water nearby—possibly a river, stream, lake, or bay in front of the site.

Wooden beams, simple furniture, and all-day light make this a truly natural home. Remodeled barns such as this are increasingly popular, but are only suitable for those with the time, energy, and finances to invest.

For good feng shui, your home should be backed by hills, on a gentle slope facing slow-moving water. Such sites can be hard to find. An alternative might be this peaceful house, standing in its own space, sheltered by trees that are not oppressively close.

CREATING A

24

**SPACE
AND
HARMONY**

56

LIGHT

HARMONIOUS HOME

132
**LIVING
THINGS**

112
**SCENTS
AND
SOUND**

76
COLOR

SPACE AND

HARMONY

The starting point for a harmonious home has to be the building itself—and the spaces or rooms within it. Each room is a basic shell, which you can plan, design, decorate, and furnish to suit your needs. Your home is the place in which you live, work, relax, eat, store possessions, and socialize; the way you plan your space will reflect all these activities. But a really healthy and harmonious home should also be a happy one, where family members can relax and enjoy their surroundings and not be afraid of making a mess!

Balance and harmony are essential both to health and good interior design, and are often the result of combining the practical and the aesthetic. Your space has to be designed to work for those who will use it. But it also needs to be a pleasant, healthy, and attractive environment, one that enhances physical and spiritual well-being. Think, too, about change over time. Plan wisely and use your space creatively. Your home is not static; during the course of its lifetime, it will have to adapt to changing needs as the family grows up, or family members become elderly.

Within the house, you need to consider the purpose and function of each room, choosing flooring, wall decoration, fabrics, and furniture as appropriate. Rooms that have to withstand the rough-and-tumble of family life will need easy-to-clean elements and hard-wearing floorings. Keep fragile fabrics and delicate hand-printed wallpaper for less active, more restful areas.

Safety and hygiene are also important points to consider, particularly in bathrooms and kitchens. Don't forget halls and stairs in your planning either—these are the entrances into your home. They need to be warm and welcoming, hinting of good things to come in the rooms beyond.

After working out the practicalities, you can think about color for mood and atmosphere, form to create interest and movement, pattern to set style, and texture to add an extra visual and tactile dimension.

Using space harmoniously also means considering the basic design style of your property. You should plan and decorate with sympathy for the original architectural intention, restoring and renovating any interesting original features. Emphasize attractive details such as lovely fireplaces, decorative rails and ceiling moldings, arches, rustic beams, original window frames and doors, and internal shutters by the clever use of color, pattern, mirrors, and lighting. Use subtle decorating techniques to "fade" unattractive features into the background.

But avoid the temptation to overimprove. Modest houses and apartments look best decorated and furnished simply, both inside and out. Harmony is also about environmental sensitivity. Don't cover or color beautiful mellow bricks, or add windows, pillars, porticos, porches, or other features that are out of keeping with your home's façade or the façades of neighboring properties.

ESTABLISHING REQUIREMENTS

A family's demands on their home change with time. For example, as the children grow up and leave, space can be adapted or redesigned. Perhaps a bedroom that is no longer needed could become a home office.

BEFORE YOU BEGIN to plan the spaces in your home, sit down and analyze what you have—determine the purpose and function of each room and work out exactly what you want from the space. Ask yourself how it will be used, and by how many people at a time. What do you want those rooms to be? In professional design terms, this is called "taking the brief" and often involves using a pre-prepared questionnaire to establish likes and dislikes, needs and requirements, and any restrictions which might need to be taken into account, such as budget, time scale, and the need for planning permission. You can devise a list of questions and involve the rest of the family in making decisions.

THINKING ABOUT THE WHOLE HOUSE

It is often best to consider the whole house first. There is no need to be conventional about allocating rooms to particular locations. Bedrooms, for example, do not necessarily have to be upstairs, or living rooms on the ground floor.

Be flexible in your thinking. Consider using downstairs rooms for dining, family rooms, and a playroom. Upstairs, the main bedroom could also be used as an adult's living room. And if your home is becoming too small for a growing family and moving is impractical, you may think about extending and enlarging the your home, although planning an extra space needs careful thought. An

Plan carefully for your home's future needs—today's nursery may become a toddler's playroom or teenager's bedroom.

attic conversion may not be wise for noisy teenagers, nor is it practical for elderly relatives. Instead, an attic conversion might be ideal for a study or office, an adult's bedroom, or a living room—especially if there are fantastic views.

If your house has an attached garage, you could convert it into a work or hobbies room, or a playroom. It could become a practical study/office, maybe with separate access, or even a dining room, allowing you to redesign your existing living room.

Ultimately you will make the choices that are most appropriate for you—influenced often by light, space, positioning, and the feel that you get from individual rooms.

EASY FLOW

Planning rooms also needs thought and analysis. You need to consider the basic characteristics of each room—its size, shape, and orientation (the direction it faces). You also need to think about how much natural daylight it receives as well as the state of the framework and how easy it will be to make alterations.

Aim to create a comfortable "traffic flow" in each room, avoiding any awkward obstructions, providing good storage space, and creating an environment that is positive and workable according to the purpose and function of the room. When planning, think about how doors and windows open, and where to place chairs, beds, sofas, and other furniture so they do not obstruct flow through the room.

MULTI-FUNCTIONAL ROOMS

In today's homes, with restricted space, you may need to plan some rooms to be multifunctional, or to use a feng shui term, split-functional. This can be harder than planning a single-purpose room. You will need to be flexible, especially when choosing furniture, storage, and surfaces in order to make sure they will suit the different activities taking place.

One room, for instance, may have to be both spare bedroom and home office. Think about a convertible sofa, which will provide both seating and sleeping facilities. You will need office storage, but also something that can incorporate clothes for an overnight guest. A desk may have to serve as a dresser as well. Floor, wall, and window treatments will have to be more practical and suitable for multipurpose use than in a conventional bedroom.

THINK AHEAD

Planning space also involves thinking ahead. What begins now as a nursery may, over the years, have to evolve into a bedroom for a teenager. Your kitchen may now contain only basic items; in the future you may be adding more equipment as your needs change.

KNOCKING DOWN WALLS

Think carefully before knocking down interior walls and creating a vast open-plan space—this may be a wonderful design for a loft, where the essential look is of one large multipurpose area, but do consider your own lifestyle, and how much privacy you want. In an open-plan area everything will be on view.

Practical tips

Before you start any decorating or furnishing, check that the structure of your home is sound, and that all the "services"—plumbing and electrical outlets in particular—are safe and conveniently located. You may need to call in experts to advise you.

Make sure that you deal with or repair any structural problems such as condensation, worm- or insect-infested wood, rot, rotting woodwork, and creaking or damaged floorboards before you begin adding color schemes or using surface treatments.

Creative salvage

If you have interesting original features such as tiled or stone floors, iron fireplaces, or old bathroom and kitchen items that you don't want to keep, don't throw them away. Someone else may want them. Consider creative salvage: selling them to a specialized salvage company that will be able to remove the items carefully—and may give you some money to add to your budget.

THE ANCIENT ART OF PLACEMENT

The setting sun relaxes energy levels, making a west-facing room calm and peaceful. Touches of red boost fire energy and prevent stagnation.

INTERIOR DESIGN uses the practical planning of space, suitable storage, and decoration to create harmony in the home. Feng shui also places great emphasis on harmony and efficiency, and on organizing space to provide a healthy flow of energy to encourage, boost, or stimulate various aspects of your life. Some aspects of feng shui are complex, and those who want to organize their homes strictly according to feng shui principles sometimes call in professional consultants to advise them.

In feng shui the type and siting of a property, as well as its surroundings, are extremely important and can have positive or negative effects on energy flow and on the occupants of the house. Some principles may at first sight seem contradictory, but with consideration they can also make a great deal of sense. For instance, a small house on a dead-end street may appear to epitomize calm and tranquility; a feng shui practitioner, however, might argue that such a setup could block energy flows, leading to stagnation.

Orientation, too, the direction in which a home or room faces, is also of great significance, particularly in the Compass school of feng shui, which believes that specific points of the compass exert profound influences that should be

Sunlight activates or boosts energy, so choose rooms accordingly. An east-facing room, for instance, makes a good kitchen. Healthy plants encourage well-being.

Ancient luo pan compass

considered when planning space. South, for instance, represents heat, midsummer, or midday, so any south-facing room boosts energy and should be used for that purpose. A south-facing room, for instance, would make a good play-room or a place for midday parties. By contrast, north is a colder direction, encouraging inwardness and quiet contemplation. A north-facing room might therefore make an ideal study or a library. East is the direction of the rising sun, bringing morning or rising energy; such a direction might be good for a kitchen, where the energy can be cooked into the food, a breakfast room, or a child's bedroom. West is the direction of the setting sun,

and where energy flows relax; try to use west-facing rooms for relaxation, perhaps to create a peaceful living room for calm family or social gatherings.

BOOSTING LIFE CHANCES

According to feng shui, different areas of your home relate to particular aspects of your life, namely: wealth, fame, relationships, ancestors, health, children, knowledge, career, and benefactors. By organizing your space with these in mind, either by allocating rooms to particular areas of the house, or by organizing the space within individual rooms themselves, you can boost or influence these different aspects of your

life. Always keep in mind that balance and harmony are the ultimate aims of feng shui.

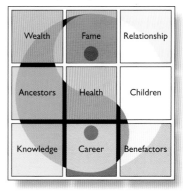

Nine areas of the bagua

4	9	2
3	5	7
8	1	6

In feng shui there are nine important life aspects, which can be related to different areas of the home. Health comes when these aspects are in balance.

Feng shui practitioners might argue that a dead-end street is not a good place to live because it traps energy, causing stagnation. Others might see it as a calm haven.

Divided into the nine principal life aspects, a bagua "template" (above) can be placed over a plan of your home showing how the aspects and areas relate. Working from this, you can organize your home to influence your life chances. The template is always laid with the front door in the knowledge, career, or benefactor area (far left).

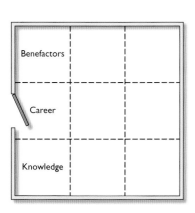

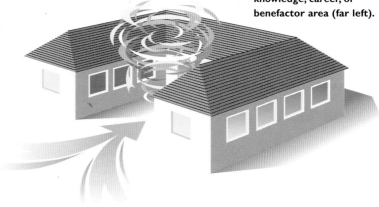

TAKING MEASUREMENTS

CREATING A HARMONIOUS space requires careful planning. Once you have decided on the purpose and function of your rooms, and know what you are going to want in the way of furniture, storage, and so on, you need to produce floor plans to scale. With these you can plan your use of space in a practical and efficient way.

In addition to making a floor plan, you can also produce a wall plan, known as an elevation. This is essentially a flat plan, which also shows the accurate positioning of doors, windows, fireplaces, radiators, baseboards, moldings, and so on. Even though the plan is not shown in perspective, you can use it to plan three-dimensionally, deciding how to treat windows, built-in features such as shelves or closets, and even where you are going to site wall lights.

Your plan will be invaluable. You can take it with you when you are buying furniture, or choosing materials for any color schemes.

You can use it to plot the position of so-called services—plumbing, lighting, telephone wires—so they harmonize with their surroundings and your furniture, and to decide on any structural work, which should obviously be done before decorating.

Measuring up

To measure accurately you will need: a good steel tape (fabric ones stretch in use)—preferably a 6-foot long retractable one; a plumbline so you can measure vertically; and a carpenter's level to find the true horizontal. You will also need scrap paper, a pencil, and possibly a calculator. A willing partner to hold the other end of the tape and double-check your calculations can also be an asset. You may also need a stepladder and flashlight.

Gather up all the equipment you will need to make a master plan before you begin to organize your home; the process will prevent mistakes later.

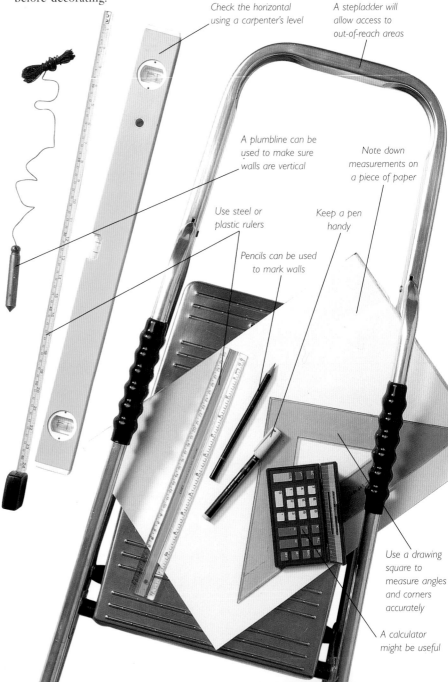

Check the horizontal using a carpenter's level

A stepladder will allow access to out-of-reach areas

A plumbline can be used to make sure walls are vertical

Note down measurements on a piece of paper

Use steel or plastic rulers

Keep a pen handy

Pencils can be used to mark walls

Use a drawing square to measure angles and corners accurately

A calculator might be useful

MAKING THE PLAN

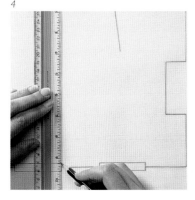

MAKE a quick sketch of the room on plain paper. Follow the shape of the room, including recesses and projections such as fireplaces. Indicate doors, and which way they open, as well as windows, radiators, built-in furniture, or appliances such as bathtub or stove. Include pipes, electric sockets, and light fixtures.

Measure everything accurately, and jot figures on the sketch plan. Start measuring in one corner of the room, and work around systematically until you are back where you began. Keep the tape taut, and always measure on the true horizontal and vertical, using your level and plumbline to check the accuracy.

Think three-dimensionally and measure the width and height of the walls, taking your measurements at several different places because walls are rarely perfectly rectangular or square. Measure diagonally from corner to corner across each wall as an extra check.

Once you have accurate measurements, translate them onto a scale floor plan and wall elevations, by drawing up accurate plans on graph paper. Indicate the

Make a plan by first drawing a sketch (1). Then take accurate measurements, noting these on the sketch before drawing a plan on graph paper (2). Trace the plan on plain paper and make overlays for lighting before tracing the final plan (3 and 4).

thicknesses of walls and show how windows are inset and which way they open. Include the thicknesses of doors. Use a drawing square to achieve perfect angles, and a compass to indicate curves such as door swings.

Choose a scale to suit yourself and the size of the room—the usual scale is 1:20, 1:25, 1:50, or 1:100—the plan, therefore, will be 20, 25, 50, or 100 times smaller than the floor or wall itself—and all measurements should be reduced to the same scale. It also makes sense to draw floor plans and wall elevations in similar scale, so they relate to each other.

Finally, trace your plan from the graph paper onto plain paper. You can then make tracing-paper overlays for any lighting plans or window treatments and lay them over the master plan.

Once you are satisfied that the plan is neat and accurate, ink in the lines firmly, so you can see them clearly through the tracing paper, then trace the complete plan. Don't forget to indicate the scale and compass orientation on the plan. Do not write measurements on a scale plan, as this defeats the object of the exercise. You can photocopy the tracing-paper drawing, using it like a negative, if you want a more robust plan—and extra copies.

FITTING IN THE FURNITURE

YOU CAN USE your floor plan to decide how to position your furniture and appliances, such as bathroom or kitchen equipment. Measure each piece of furniture carefully, whether it is already in your home or is something you are buying. Then, working to the same scale as your plan, cut out the shapes on graph paper or cardboard to make templates, and move them around on your floor plan. This type of planning is particularly useful if you are moving, but it is also a good way of planning existing space.

It is much easier to work with small pieces of paper and cardboard, than to heave furniture around.

Remember to allow enough room to open windows, drawers, and doors. Bear in mind the space you need for moving furniture, perhaps when making beds or cleaning, or for pushing chairs back from desks and tables. Plan to use space in such a way that people can move easily through and around the room, without being hampered by awkwardly positioned pieces of furniture. Take particular care with some multipurpose items such as convertible sofas, desks

Pieces of colored paper, cut to size as furniture templates, can be moved and positioned on your floor plan.

with drop-down flaps, and folding tables. Measure and template them carefully, open and closed, to see how much space they take up in both positions.

When positioning furniture, you should always aim for a feeling of harmony. Avoid "confrontational" situations when you open the door to a room. Don't place a couch in such a way that the door bangs the arm or back; it disrupts energy and causes irritation. Feng shui practitioners also advise against placing chair backs facing doors, as this disrupts the flow of energy into and around a room. Beds and toilets should not be visible.

Avoid placing desks and other work surfaces in dark corners facing the wall; instead place them under a window, at an angle, or facing forward into the room. In this way, you will be looking into the room, rather than literally feeling hemmed into a corner. You are aiming always for a smooth movement of energy and traffic flow through the room.

Once you are certain that everything is placed well, and that you can use the room with ease and comfort, check to make sure that lighting, plumbing, and other services fit into the room harmoniously. Then use your templates to trace the shapes and positions of your furniture onto your plan.

PLANNING AN EXTRA VISUAL DIMENSION
Designing a room is not just about fitting in furniture; it also involves considering the forms or shapes that will

surround you and that can provide an extra visual dimension in their own right.

Contrasting forms—ovals, circles, and curves—combined with square and oblong forms can change one's perception of the shape and perspective of a room. A curved seating arrangement, for instance, will bring a feeling of harmony and interest into a squarish room; an L-shaped arrangement of furniture can divide a long, thin area and create a split-purpose room. In the dining room, an oval or circular dining table will complement a long, slim sideboard or storage units. In the bedroom, a circular bed can add interest and offset the rigid lines of closets or chests. Such forms add extra visual interest to any shape of room.

You need not confine contrast to the horizontal plane; think three-dimensionally as well, varying the heights of furniture as well as their shapes. In high-ceilinged rooms you can use different items of furniture to offset the height, but in low-ceilinged rooms avoid tall pieces of furniture. In a kitchen or dining room you could combine a hutch with a simple refectory-style or circular table. In the bedroom, an unusually shaped headboard will add extra interest to a wall. You can use some interesting drapes above a bed, but avoid any sense of hemming yourself in. You can also add interest by using contrast; for example, you might place a circular or oval mirror above a square fireplace or between two tall, slim windows.

A tall, dramatic, four-poster bed sets off a high-ceilinged room to perfection, while the round mirror above the square fireplace adds contrast.

Well-planned furniture placement allows for easy, flowing movement through and around a room.

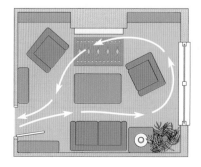

STREAMLINING YOUR HOME

IN BOTH FENG SHUI AND INTE-RIOR DESIGN, a healthy approach to space involves avoiding clutter. We all acquire possessions; they are an integral part of our lives. But too much clutter and disorder can bring not only specific health hazards, but also tension, anxiety, and depression, a sense of not being able to cope. According to feng shui, too, excess clutter disrupts the flow of energy, causing stagnation and tiredness; sorting your possessions and clearing out clutter from time to time can have a very refreshing effect.

At the same time, however, the things we own have practical uses, and are often objects of beauty. Creating harmony therefore involves good storage, and using available space creatively. From a practical point of view, it makes sense to store items you use frequently, in the areas where you use them. China, flatware, linen, glasses, and so on need to be stored close to the table for example, perhaps in a sideboard or cupboards. Clothes, shoes, handbags, and accessories are best stored in the bedroom, but overcoats, hefty boots, and sports equipment may be best kept close to the front or back door.

STORAGE SOLUTIONS

Closed storage closets and chests or drawer units often provide ideal storage solutions. You can put possessions away neatly, but also have quick access to things when you need them. Some decorative items can be displayed on open shelves as an integral part of your decorative house schemes adding color and pattern.

Some homes, however, have limited space for built-in or free-standing furniture. If this is the case, look at your home again. There may be many places where you can install suitable storage, which you have not yet considered. A window seat, for example, with a lift-up top can be used to store things like magazines, newspapers, or games. Or you can store clothes or toys in drawers under the bed.

Think about building shelves in unusual places—tailored to fit into the wall at the side of a bay window, for example, or on each side of a sash window. None of these solutions will take up much floor space, yet the overall effect will be sleek and streamlined.

USING SPACE CREATIVELY

Most homes contain usable space if you look for it—both overhead and underfoot. It may be practical to board over the joists in the attic, install a glazed skylight and electricity, and use this space for storing items that are not used every day, or to make full use of a cellar. Remember, however, to check and reassess the contents regularly. But there is no reason to tuck away frequently used items. Ceiling racks, for instance, once used in kitchens to air clothes and dry herbs, can be used either for their original purpose or to hang tools, sports equipment, or towels. They can also be used for hanging baskets or attractive pots and pans adding a decorative, as well as purely prac-tical, touch. You might also consider mounting the traditional wooden plate draining rack on the wall for storing plates, cups, and saucers.

There is often usable space above a door or window for installing a cupboard, or you may be able to add extra shelves inside existing wall cabinets for storing infrequently used items such as Christmas decorations, picnic baskets, and so on. And if there are moldings in your house, you could install a wider shelf above them to display or store attractive china and porcelain. Another popular and traditional method of storage is the Shaker-style peg rack—a wall-mounted rail with projecting pegs that hold a variety of objects—clothes, fabric bags filled with items, even dining chairs!

A cheap and easy way of removing clutter from rooms is to screw simple hooks to the edge of

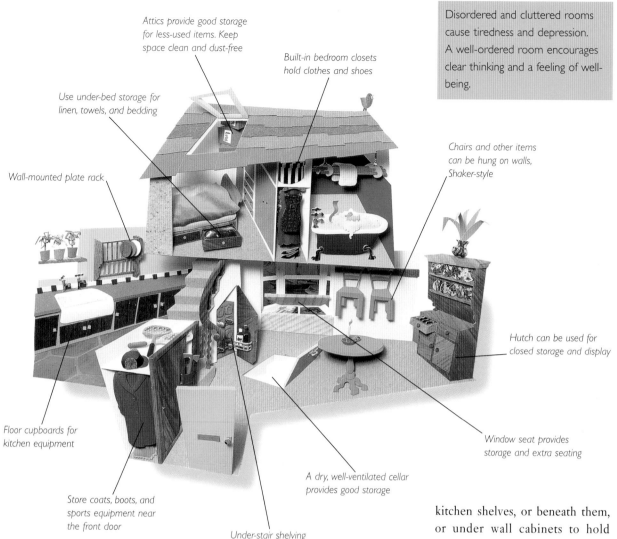

Attics provide good storage for less-used items. Keep space clean and dust-free

Built-in bedroom closets hold clothes and shoes

Use under-bed storage for linen, towels, and bedding

Wall-mounted plate rack

Chairs and other items can be hung on walls, Shaker-style

Hutch can be used for closed storage and display

Floor cupboards for kitchen equipment

Window seat provides storage and extra seating

Store coats, boots, and sports equipment near the front door

A dry, well-ventilated cellar provides good storage

Under-stair shelving or cupboard

Home should be an escape from the chaos of daily life, so use all potential storage space to remove clutter and create a relaxed environment.

Possessions don't have to be tucked away in dark corners. Suspend pots and pans from a ceiling rack and hang your summer hats, Shaker style, from a pegged trellis (far left).

Constant clearing up is exhausting. Wicker baskets stacked in open wooden shelving (left) can provide a simple and healthy solution for vegetables and fruit.

kitchen shelves, or beneath them, or under wall cabinets to hold cups, pitchers, and other items with a handle. They can also be used in garden sheds, or in a child's room for hanging toys.

Other places can be adapted for storage. The area under the stairs can be shelved and used for storing wine racks, bottles, and tools. The backs of built-in cupboard doors can be equipped with hanging hooks, racks, or plastic containers. This type of arrangement works well in the kitchen, where canned and dry goods need cool, dark storage. Make sure doors and hinges are strong enough to take the extra weight. If necessary, cut existing shelves into an elongated U-shape to accommodate storage on the back of the door. If cupboards are deep, install a light that comes on as the door is opened.

PLANNING FROM THE INSIDE OUT

Simple, adjustable shelving can hold a variety of possessions.

YOU CAN PROVIDE instant storage in many different ways: free-standing pieces, flexible adjustable shelving, and built-in storage, which you can build yourself or hire a professional carpenter to construct. But before you go hunting for storage space, work out exactly what you want to store, as well as its size and weight, and then fit storage to needs. In an ideal world, storage would be planned from the inside out so that you organized it around what you need to store.

Measure everything you want to store—its height, weight, and density—and relate your measurements to the width, depth, height of existing drawers, shelves, closets, and cupboards. In the bedroom, for example, consider how much space your clothes need, hanging or folded, as well as considering other items that might be kept in the room such as luggage, handbags, accessories, and so on.

With dining area storage, you will need to check the dimensions of serving dishes and stacks of plates, the space needed for glassware, bottles, and decanters. Storage requirements in the living room may be very extensive; you may need to find homes for a variety of possessions from books and glasses to CDs, music system, and television. Books in particular come in a multitude of sizes and can be very heavy. Adjustable shelving is often the most practical solution, supported on brackets that fit into a special slotted angle screwed to the wall. Such shelving can be used on its own in recesses, or combined with chests or cupboards to create "closed storage" or built-in units for large items such as a television or hi-fi system.

Glass shelving works very well and can be used in living rooms, bedrooms, and bathrooms. It is functional and can be very decorative, particularly if it is well lit to highlight possessions you want to display as well as store.

INSTANT STORAGE

Today there is an enormous choice of instant storage available—much of which is extremely attractive, providing a stylish as well as a practical solution to the question of clutter. You can use clear plastic containers for clothes, shoes, linen, and small accessories; metal and wire minimalist-style items that look particularly good in hi-tech kitchens or home offices; wicker and cane pieces that have an attractive rustic look; colorful plastic stacking storage boxes. These are ideal for playrooms or a teenage bedroom and can even encourage neatness.

Instant storage also includes folding cupboard containers and boxes for filing systems, portable stacking racks, fabric containers for items such as jewelry, tie-up laundry and linen storage, and decorative "tents" to disguise clothes-hanging spaces.

Display shelves such as glass or wicker containers can be used decoratively to display colorful and interesting items such as legumes and pasta in the kitchen, attractive soaps and creams in the bathroom, or costume jewelry in the bedroom.

Baskets can be attractive and are also easily portable containers. Simple hooks, peg racks, and pegboards together with their displayed items also provide interesting visual features.

If you need "closed" storage to keep out dust and dirt, consider linen baskets and boxes in the bedroom and bathroom, adapt tool boxes, or make use of needlework and hobby baskets. Suitcases, cabin trunks, sturdy ottomans with lift-up tops, wicker hampers, and large theatrical carts hold an enormous amount and are interesting objects.

But before you rush out to choose from the huge selection available, be sure that your projected storage solutions are optimal—both in terms of meeting your actual storage needs within the available space and in terms of overall style.

Fabric shelves, hanging from a pole, are colorful and space-saving, but not always practical if they are overloaded. Before spending money on storage, make sure it meets your needs.

A custom-designed closet can answer your specific storage needs. Build one yourself or hire a professional carpenter.

Drawers and shelves can be fitted under and around hanging racks. Shoes can be stored under dresses and coats

Remember the extras— weekend bags and sports equipment, for example— and plan extra shelves. They are sure to be filled in no time!

CREATING AN ENTRANCE

Your hall is one of the most important areas in the house. It is usually the point of entry into the home, so it should be welcoming and have impact. It is also the connecting area to all other rooms and needs to be planned so the transition to other rooms is easy and harmonious. You need good access and ease of movement through to the other rooms; consider using color or pattern to make visual links between the hall and rooms beyond. If you have a tall, narrow hall, think about using mirrors and color or pattern to improve the proportions from a visual perspective.

Plan for the number of doors in the hall, particularly considering which way they open. Make sure there is good air circulation—you may need to rehang a door to make circulation easier—but avoid drafts. A screen or closed porch can help to prevent them.

Most halls are not rooms in their own right, so plan storage carefully in this area to avoid clutter. Create a specific place for letters, keys, clothes brushes, and so on; and a practical and ordered space for outdoor clothes. If you decide to put a telephone in the hall, try to organize the space so you can sit comfortably; have a shelf or table where you can write messages, and somewhere to store telephone directories. A hall mirror will add dimension and light, as well as allow you to check your appearance before you leave the house.

In feng shui a red door brings luck into the home. Entrances and hallways are often neglected, but, as the way into your home, they should be bright, warm, and welcoming, for you as for others.

FENG SHUI HALLWAYS

In feng shui the entrance to the house has enormous importance, as it is here that both people and energy enter the home. Your front door should be bright, well maintained, and welcoming. If it is too large in relation to the hall, energy escapes; however, this can be counteracted by hanging wind chimes at the entrance. Flowering or green shrubs in the porch or on the front door step are attractive and also encourage well-being. If your hall or corridors are small, narrow, or dark, hang a mirror on one wall to give a sense of greater width and to boost energy flow. If your hallway runs directly through to a back door, feng shui practitioners believe that energy will rush directly through and out of the house; a mirror placed at the end of the hall can prevent this from happening. Landings should be light and airy, and furniture and storage kept to a minimum.

> **Health point**
> Make sure hall and stairs are well lit and free from drafts.

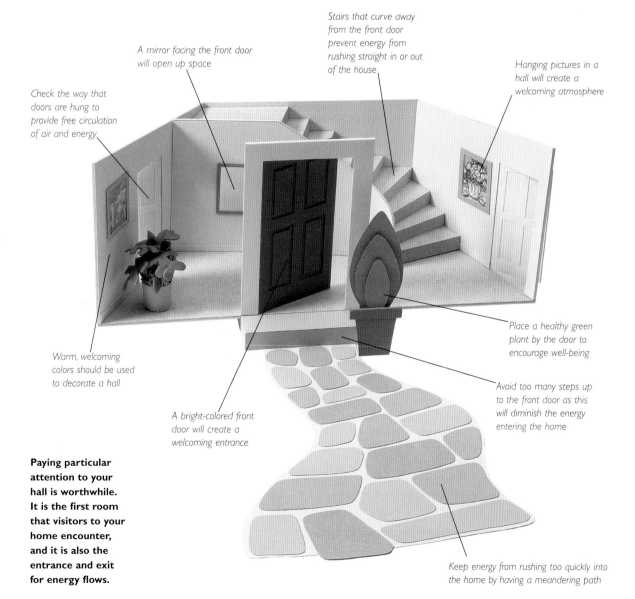

Check the way that doors are hung to provide free circulation of air and energy

A mirror facing the front door will open up space

Stairs that curve away from the front door prevent energy from rushing straight in or out of the house

Hanging pictures in a hall will create a welcoming atmosphere

Warm, welcoming colors should be used to decorate a hall

A bright-colored front door will create a welcoming entrance

Place a healthy green plant by the door to encourage well-being

Avoid too many steps up to the front door as this will diminish the energy entering the home

Keep energy from rushing too quickly into the home by having a meandering path

Paying particular attention to your hall is worthwhile. It is the first room that visitors to your home encounter, and it is also the entrance and exit for energy flows.

THE DINING ROOM

Eating and drinking are important. This traditional dining room has a sumptuous feel conducive to a dinner-party atmosphere. Candles on an oval table encourage socializing, while red-colored walls create warmth and stimulate appetite.

By contrast, this modern living space, which contains both dining and living room, is much calmer. Pale walls, skylights, and a total absence of clutter combine to produce a simple, light, spacious environment for everyday meals and small gatherings.

Dining chairs should be comfortable so that diners will be happy seated at the table and can enjoy their meal.

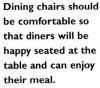

A DINING ROOM might be the hub of the home—a separate room from the kitchen, and the place where family meals and entertaining take place, with good wine, food, and conversation. If this is the case, plan to create a cozy, intimate ambience, but be sure to consider the practicalities needed for serving hot food and drinks.

The room should contain a table large enough for family and guests. Round tables encourage a more harmonious eating and socializing environment where no one person feels excluded at one corner or another, so consider this in your planning, perhaps choosing one that extends to an oval. Folding or extending tables are useful when space is limited. Choose comfortable chairs that relate well to the height of the table, allowing people to be seated without hitting knees or elbows. Think carefully, too, about the amount of space needed to push chairs easily back from the table without knocking into other items.

If space allows, create a separate space for serving food. This should be as close to the kitchen door as possible, or under an opening cut in the wall separating the kitchen and dining space. A portable trolley is a practical alternative if space is limited.

Plan storage for all the items you need for serving, eating, and drinking. If the room is a split-function room, possibly doubling as a dining room and study, use a screen, bead curtain, or something similar to divide the room into two.

FENG SHUI DINING ROOMS

For feng shui practitioners, as for anyone else, eating is an important activity, so the dining room should be planned with this in mind. The aim is to create a harmonious and good feeling among the diners.

Furniture should be kept to a minimum—perhaps only a dining table, chairs, and sideboard. Here, too, oval or circular dining tables are recommended because they nurture harmony and balance, both within the room and among the diners. The shape supports the energy flow and has what is known as a "gathering" influence; rectangular tables are best kept for more controlled situations such as business meetings. Natural wood is recommended for both tables and other surfaces.

Ideally, eating and food preparation should be separated, so the dining room and kitchen are apart from each other. If this is not the case, you can create a separation using a room divider or perhaps a screen.

Mirrors can be used to good advantage in the dining room—by reflecting food and diners, they effectively increase a sense of abundance and well-being. They stimulate energy flow, which in turn stimulates conversation.

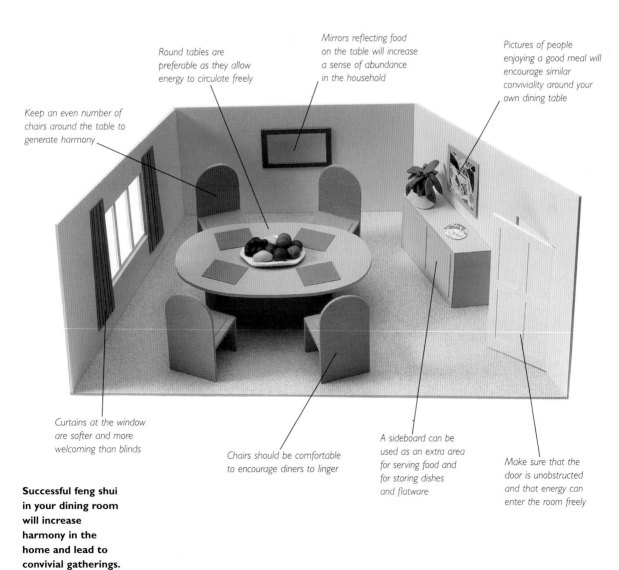

Round tables are preferable as they allow energy to circulate freely

Mirrors reflecting food on the table will increase a sense of abundance in the household

Pictures of people enjoying a good meal will encourage similar conviviality around your own dining table

Keep an even number of chairs around the table to generate harmony

Curtains at the window are softer and more welcoming than blinds

Chairs should be comfortable to encourage diners to linger

A sideboard can be used as an extra area for serving food and for storing dishes and flatware

Make sure that the door is unobstructed and that energy can enter the room freely

Successful feng shui in your dining room will increase harmony in the home and lead to convivial gatherings.

LIVING SPACES
THE LIVING ROOM

THESE DAYS, a formal drawing room is very rare; instead living rooms are more likely to be used for family living. Sometimes called sitting rooms, they need to be versatile because so many activities are likely to take place in them. You need therefore to plan carefully for all requirements.

Comfortable seating is the first consideration—this may mean flexible modular units, two or three sofas, some extra chairs, maybe some folding pieces or floor cushions. The amount of furniture depends on the size and shape of the room, but avoid creating a cluttered environment. Encourage members of the family to try out seating to make sure it meets their needs. From a practical point of view, think about the safety aspects, particularly in terms of fire and ease of cleaning. You may also need to include small tables for lamps and other items.

Storage will depend on how you are going to use the room, but the living room will probably need to incorporate CDs, cassettes, and video plus television, so you will need to include these in your plans when looking at your use of space. Any large pieces of furniture should be placed some distance from the seating and the fireplace.

The furnishings in the living room may reflect the style of the room, but considerations such as comfort should also be primary.

Health point

Avoid unsafe upholstery and materials such as inflammable foam in couches and chairs. Put a fireguard in front of an open fire.

Back problems are only too common, so good seating should be a priority. Choose chairs according to need—firm-backed chairs that support your back when eating or working, a comfortable but supportive armchair with arm rests for relaxing.

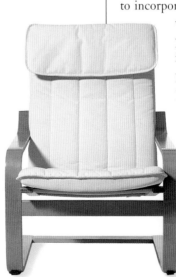

FENG SHUI LIVING
ROOM
Southwest-facing rooms are favored here because this direction is said to encourage good relationships, but within the room your aim should be to create a spacious, comfortable, and relaxed atmosphere. A circular arrangement for seating promotes relaxation and allows a smooth circulation of energy. For relaxation, too, it is important to avoid clutter.

Create a balanced seating arrangement, possibly grouped around a table, with separate pieces slightly angled rather than positioned directly opposite each other, which can be confrontational. The shape and size of your seating can vary, provided the overall effect is balanced. In a particularly large room, you may be able to separate the room into different areas, perhaps one for conversation or family discussions with chairs in a companionable circle, and another area for television or games.

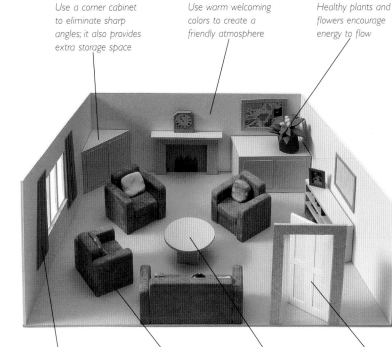

Use a corner cabinet to eliminate sharp angles; it also provides extra storage space

Use warm welcoming colors to create a friendly atmosphere

Healthy plants and flowers encourage energy to flow

Choose curtains that harmonize with other furnishings in the room

Chairs placed in a circular arrangement create a more harmonious atmosphere

Round tables allow energy to flow uninterrupted

Energy can flow freely into an uncluttered area of the room

How you place your furniture in your living room is very important in feng shui. A simple rearrangement of the chairs in the seating area and adding a round table rather than a rectangular version can create more satisfactory energy flows.

A confrontational seating arrangement with occupants directly facing one another

An angular occasional table prevents energy from circulating

A door opening onto the back of the sofa is irksome and blocks energy flows

Coping with the television
Television can be a favored source of family entertainment and information; it can also, and frequently does, create problems, disrupting conversations and causing tensions. Its presence can have an almost hypnotic effect. For these reasons, it is advisable to make the television as unobtrusive as possible, perhaps even placing it in closed or open-shelved storage when it is not being used.

LIVING SPACES
THE
KITCHEN

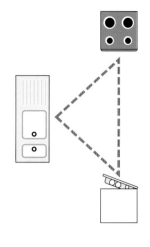

FOR MANY PEOPLE the kitchen is the heart of the home, and one of the most important rooms in the house. It is here that food is cooked, for entertainment and family meals; it may also be the place where the family gathers, where children do their homework, and a variety of tasks are carried out. For others, the kitchen may be less active and more stream-lined, but it still remains fundamental to the home.

You need to analyze your kitchen carefully before you plan how to organize it, bearing in mind how you are going to use it. What-ever solutions you choose, a kitchen must be safe, and there should be separate areas for dif-ferent tasks such as preparing food, cooking, washing dishes, eating, laundry, and so on, so that the individual functions do not conflict with each other.

All kitchens need a stove, sink, refrigerator/freezer and other food storage facilities, work surfaces, and space to use and store kitchen equipment and utensils. You may also need to put a dishwasher in the kitchen, and a washing machine and dryer if your home does not have a separate utility room. If the space is large enough, you may want to have a table and chairs, or a breakfast bar and stools, for snacks and quick meals.

In order to prepare, cook, and store food in the best way possi-ble, you need to be able to move and work efficiently and safely between the areas where you are going to carry out the different tasks. Many people recommend a so-called work triangle so you can move easily between the food storage area, work surface, and stove. Different forms of this arrangement can be used in a variety of kitchen shapes and sizes.

For a healthy kitchen, all sur-faces, particularly stove top, sink, draining boards, and work surfaces, must be clean. Ceramic tiles, marble, enamel, and stainless steel surfaces are all easy to keep clean.

The work triangle shows placement of kitchen appliances for maximum efficiency.

With easy-to-clean work surfaces, good storage, and sharp knives out of reach, this kitchen/ breakfast room is safe and functional.

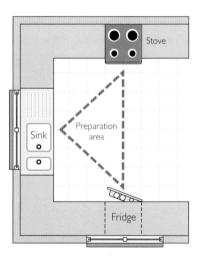

Keeping the stove
away from the sink is
ideal feng shui; here
it is also sited on an
island, allowing the
cook to be relaxed
and see all around
the kitchen when
cooking.

FENG SHUI

In feng shui, the kitchen is not only the place where food is stored and prepared, it is associated with healing and well-being, and may also reflect or influence the wealth or status of the family. It should be kept clean and uncluttered, and the positioning of objects should encourage a good energy flow; rounded edges for kitchen surfaces are recommended, rather than sharp edges or angles, which can cause disharmony.

The positioning of kitchen equipment, particularly the stove, reflects the principles of the Five Elements. For harmony, therefore, the stove, as a fire element, is placed some distance from the refrigerator and sink, both of which are water elements. In a feng shui kitchen, the stove is the most important appliance of all. It can be placed in the center of the kitchen, so that the cook looks out into all areas of the kitchen and is never startled while cooking. If, for any reason, you need to place your stove against a wall, and your back therefore faces the door while you are cooking, you should hang a mirror above the stove so you can look into the room as you work.

Health point

Keep work surfaces and utensils spotlessly clean. Store sharp and heavy objects, such as knives, scissors, and pots, in cabinets. Avoid slippery floor surfaces. Keep children away from stoves and point pan handles away from stove edges. Check food regularly to make sure it is fresh.

All sharp objects should be kept hidden; knives could be kept in a block or drawer

The best place for the sink is under a window. This sink is also positioned away from the stove, avoiding a clash of fire and water elements

Good energy flows are maintained if surfaces are uncluttered

An exhaust fan will help to remove excess heat and damp from the kitchen and keep them from spreading to other areas of the house

Use shelves to display your favorite attractive china to add welcoming color to the room

Cork is an ideal flooring—it is warm both to walk on and in color, and is easy to clean

Cabinets should be used to store all kitchen equipment, avoiding clutter, and should be kept closed

Following a few simple feng shui rules when designing the kitchen can influence the health, wealth, and harmony of family members.

CLEANSING
SPACES
BATHROOMS

BATHROOMS SHOULD be pleasant places, where you can start the day in a positive mood and end it in a relaxed frame of mind. The way you plan space here must reflect individual needs—whether the family contains small children, or elderly people, for instance—and the size and number of pieces of equipment such as bathtub, washbasin, and toilet.

Your house may have just one bathroom, or there may be separate areas for the toilet and the bathtub. You may have more than one bathroom, in which case each room may have slightly different purposes. A guest bedroom, for instance, may have a connecting bathroom that is rarely used.

No matter how many bathrooms you have in the house, you will need clever planning in order to fit in all the necessary items and to maintain a neat and uncluttered environment. This is one area where paper planning and careful measuring can be very useful. It can be particularly helpful to plot the pipe locations on your original plan, to make sure new basins, bathtubs, and so on are positioned as efficiently as possible.

In a fairly large bathroom, you may have room for a separate shower. You may also have space for a shower in another part of the house. If neither of these is possible, you may choose to install a shower over the bathtub. Showers are refreshing and efficient, but it is as well to resist the temptation to replace a bathtub with a shower, because there are times when you will want to relax and indulge in a long soak.

Bathrooms lend themselves to clutter, which should always be avoided. Think about using wall-mounted cupboards as "closed" storage, above the toilet or basin—at head height, of course—or shelves for display purposes. You may also be able to use space around the bathtub, that is often shut off by fixed panels by adding panels that can be opened and closed.

Windows are an important feature for fresh air as well as natural light. Sheer curtains (below) or opaque glass (above) will let in light while maintaining privacy.

Placing plants in the bathroom helps create a lush, relaxing atmosphere. The fern family offers a variety of plants that thrive in high humidity and shade.

FENG SHUI By definition, bathrooms are associated with the water element and are considered to be difficult rooms in feng shui. Water is obviously cleansing, and the two rooms are primarily concerned with removing waste, but water and elimination can also flush or drain away energy, well-being, and possibly even wealth. The correct positioning of the bathroom can do much to counteract this process. Feng shui practitioners would advise against placing a bathroom in the center of the house, next to the kitchen, or opposite the front door, because all these positionings cause energy problems. Most appropriate is a bathroom against one outside wall,

preferably at the rear of the house. Alternatively, good ventilation, sunshine, and the use of mirrors to reflect energy back into the room can counteract any potential draining processes.

Where a bathroom and toilet are both in one room, it is advisable to plan some way to separate the two spaces, perhaps with a room divider. Feng shui practitioners also suggest keeping the toilet lid down to prevent the loss of wealth. The whole area should be kept clean and fresh, with wooden flooring and plants. Most feng shui practitioners advise against bathrooms connected to bedrooms in the belief that they drain energy from the bedroom.

Health point
Keep medicines and any potentially hazardous objects such as razors and nail clippers in lockable cupboards. Use nonslip mats in the shower and safety glass for the shower door.

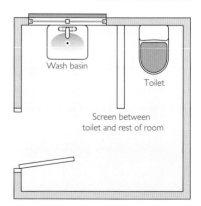

Wash basin

Toilet

Screen between toilet and rest of room

For good feng shui, try to screen the toilet from the washing area.

White touches offset the power of the cold, dark water element.

THE
BEDROOM

Choose a bed for comfort, size, and style, so it predominates but does not overwhelm the room.

Bedrooms can contain allergens: feathers and down may irritate some people, and synthetic fabrics and comforters can also cause allergic reactions. Organic cotton is considered the hypoallergenic alternative.

A bedside table should be positioned to make sure light from the lamp falls at a comfortable reading height.

YOUR BEDROOM is one of the most important rooms in the house. You are likely to spend about a third of your life in your bedroom, much of it asleep, and how you sleep and dream will deeply affect your health and life. The bedroom must meet your needs for privacy as well as for intimacy. It is where you dress, undress, store your most personal possessions, and the one place where you should be able to get away from the rest of the house and relax.

These needs should influence the way you organize your bedroom. Your first priority should be your bed. The bed should be comfortable but firm enough to promote healthy sleep, and large and strong enough to comfortably accommodate you—and your partner if you have one. You can choose a simple design, or you can make your bed a special feature, but if so, make sure it does not overwhelm the room.

For relaxation, you could also include a comfortable chair, or, if the room is large enough, a sofa or chaise lounge. You could place a sofa or lounge parallel to the foot of a double bed. You may also need a small table to hold a lamp, making sure the height is correct

Bedrooms should be designed for relaxation. The flow of energy is important, and care should be taken in the positioning of the bed.

to allow you to read comfortably in bed. Bookshelves, possibly a desk or bedside tables can all be useful, as can an attractive chest of drawers.

Some people also like to introduce a wash basin or shower into the bedroom, which can ease pressure on the family bathroom, but be careful not to impose too much on the space.

Your aim should be to create a tranquil environment so you wake up refreshed rather than tense. Be careful about how you store possessions. As the years pass, your possessions—clothes certainly—will increase, so bear this in mind when planning storage. You can create extra storage space by fitting closets on each side of a unit, chest of drawers, or dresser, and linking them with storage cupboards above that could be screwed to the ceiling. Avoid doing this over the head of the bed, however, as it can cause headaches and a feeling of being boxed in.

Space is often available under beds, where pull-out drawers can be a practical answer. In small rooms, particularly children's rooms, you could use a split-level solution, raising the bed above cupboards, a desk, or hanging space.

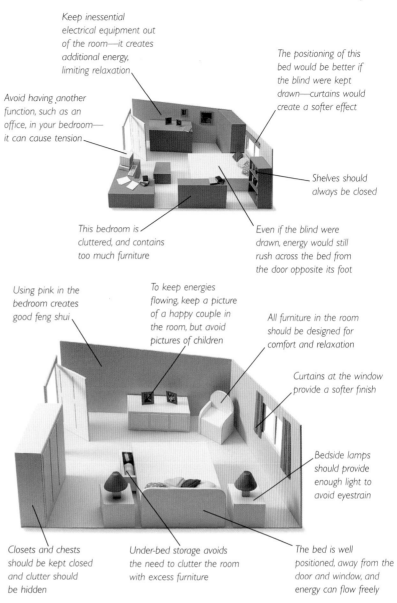

Keep inessential electrical equipment out of the room—it creates additional energy, limiting relaxation

Avoid having another function, such as an office, in your bedroom— it can cause tension

The positioning of this bed would be better if the blind were kept drawn—curtains would create a softer effect

Shelves should always be closed

This bedroom is cluttered, and contains too much furniture

Even if the blind were drawn, energy would still rush across the bed from the door opposite its foot

Using pink in the bedroom creates good feng shui

To keep energies flowing, keep a picture of a happy couple in the room, but avoid pictures of children

All furniture in the room should be designed for comfort and relaxation

Curtains at the window provide a softer finish

Bedside lamps should provide enough light to avoid eyestrain

Closets and chests should be kept closed and clutter should be hidden

Under-bed storage avoids the need to clutter the room with excess furniture

The bed is well positioned, away from the door and window, and energy can flow freely

FENG SHUI BEDROOMS
Here, too, the bedroom is the most intimate room in the home. It needs to be calm, relaxed, and safe. Clutter must be avoided. Feng shui practitioners would strongly advise against using the bedroom as an office, or even, in some cases, keeping books in the bedroom, because they can introduce a working element and therefore confusion.

Furnish to provide as uncluttered an effect as possible and avoid sharp-cornered furniture near the bed, as it can break up energy flows. Consider instead rounded edges for built-in furniture and circular bedside tables. The bed must be comfortable, ideally made of wood with linen sheets, and a natural-fiber mattress. Choosing the right bed can revitalize your energy, revive a relationship, and bring a couple back together.

Ideally, position your bed diagonally opposite the bedroom door, with the headboard against the wall. With this arrangement you will be well-grounded and free from drafts, but energy can flow freely around the room. Bedding, towels, and blankets can be stored in drawers under the bed, but avoid having storage units on either side of the head of the bed, as this will disrupt sleep and cause headaches.

Health point
For a healthy night's sleep, make sure your bed is firm, strong, and comfortable.

RESTING SPACES
CHILDREN'S BEDROOMS

A child's bedroom has to grow and develop with the child. It may begin as a nursery, used for sleeping, changing, bathing, and feeding, and evolve through various stages into an almost self-contained space for a teenager. Furniture needs to be flexible and long-lasting and storage planned with the future in mind. Decorate major surfaces so they are practical, hard-wearing, and easy to redecorate. Colors will change at each stage of the child's development. Use attractive strong pastels for the nursery stage, bold primary colors for toddlers, and more relaxing schemes when the school and homework stage is reached. Teenagers are bound to have their own ideas about decoration. Floor coverings should be practical but warm and comfortable underfoot. Paint is the most practical wall covering; woodwork and furniture can also be decorated in order to create a contrast.

Use these stage-by-stage guidelines for a bedroom that will "grow" with the child.

The nursery: plan for a crib, nursing chair, changing surface, large cupboard with hanging space, and shelves for small garments.

Toddler's room: remove the crib and nursing chair; add a junior bed, large toy box, blackboard, or other drawing surface. Put a bulletin board above the play and painting surface, formerly the changing table. Add a bookcase or shelves.

Schoolchild's room: remove junior bed, place more shelves in the closet, convert the drawing surface to a desk. Perhaps create a split level: some storage units under a bunk bed.

Study/bedroom: if you have used a bunk bed, split the bunks into single beds and place a bedside table between them. Add shelves above the desk and add a pair of director's chairs or cushions for visiting friends.

Teenage room: replace bunks and storage drawers with twin beds or a convertible bed; convert the closet to an all-hanging space; add a new chest of drawers; put in a dual-purpose desk/dresser.

Young children's bedrooms should be light, cheerful, and free of any toxic materials such as lead-based paint. All furniture, furnishings, and toys should conform to recognized safety standards.

FENG SHUI CHILDREN'S BEDROOM

Here the emphasis is on creating a place where a child or young person can escape from the ever-increasing demands of the outside world. A child's bedroom should be a place for relaxation and inspiration. For this reason, feng shui does not recommend too many primary colors; instead the emphasis is on harmonizing colors, natural-fabric toys, and a feeling of softness, light, and space. The room should contain positive and inspiring pictures, perhaps of the natural world; well-placed mobiles to keep energy moving; soft lighting; and airy window coverings. Feng shui also recommends wicker baskets or a traditional toy chest in preference to plastic stacking boxes. Synthetic floorings and fluorescent lighting should always be avoided. Colors will, of course, depend on the preferences of the child, but a yellow

Children accumulate a lot of possessions. As a toddler's room is transformed into a schoolchild's room, bunk beds can save space and provide storage.

Feng shui recommends harmonizing and soothing colors for young people's surroundings. Green plants encourage health, and all furniture and furnishings should be made from natural materials.

CREATIVE SPACES
THE WORKROOM

Working from home is stressful when space is limited. A compact work station that contains all needs but takes up little space can be a solution.

HAVING A PERMANENT work space at home is a fairly recent development. Traditionally, large houses had a library, which was usually a male preserve; more modest homes might have had a study. But the current trend toward freelancing and working at home, and the need for children to have somewhere to study away from the center of family activity, has made a private working space a more common element in many households.

Basic items of equipment might include a desk, ergonomically designed chair, storage equipment, such as shelves or filing cabinets, telephone, fax machine, computer, reference material, and desk lamps.

Planning the working space will depend very much on your needs, the type of work you do, and how much space is actually available. It will also depend on what arrangement best encourages a good work flow and boosts your energy. However, good light, well-designed chairs, unrestricted access to your equipment and reference material, plus the availability of sockets and telephone line obviously all play a part in the organization of the space.

Feng shui practitioners would also recommend a healthy green plant to help absorb pollutants, a wooden desk with curved edges, and fresh red flowers to promote clarity of thought. Ideally, the desk should

With today's emphasis on healthy living, home gyms are becoming increasingly popular. They must be planned carefully to allow for the size and weight of equipment and are best sited on a ground floor or in a garage.

be placed so your back is against the wall, providing support, and you can see whoever might come in through the door. Any workroom should be kept as clutter-free and organized as possible to prevent tension or irritation, and to encourage clear thought.

In many cases, this sort of working space has to be dual-purpose—not every home can relinquish an entire room—and sometimes a work room has to double as a spare bedroom. When this happens, it is advisable to let the most important use determine how the room is organized; also, if possible, arrange the room in such a way that two separate "zones" appear to be created.

Using ergonomically designed work stations will help to prevent back and arm ache.

Computers and health

There is increasing concern about the impact of computers on health. Keyboarding for example, can cause repetitive stress injury (RSI), which results in swelling, tenderness, and muscular spasms in any part of the arm from the elbow to the fingers. To avoid RSI, make sure you use good seating, specially designed keyboards, and the correct height of work surface. You should also take frequent breaks away from the computer screen.

ADDING
EXTRA
SPACE
SUNROOMS

ADDING AN EXTRA SPACE to a house in the form of a sunroom is a relatively recent development, but a very exciting one. Creating a sunroom or solarium can give a sense of extending your house into the outdoor environment, giving you an area of sun and light, where you can grow plants and sit and enjoy a restful environment.

But before taking such a step, you do need to work out exactly how you want to use a conservatory—as a greenhouse, summer dining extension, or even a type of play or games room. It is usually advisable to use professionals for extension work, but think carefully before calling in experts and obtain more than one financial estimate before making any decision. Alternatively, you can obtain a prefabricated solarium and do the building work yourself, but bear in mind the possibility that you may need to dig a foundation.

When planning a sunroom, remember that it can cut the light from the room or corridor from which it leads, even though it is itself a greenhouse-type building. This factor needs to be taken into account when you are choosing a site for the room and when you are choosing colors. The extension will probably become the way through to the backyard, so choose flooring with care—it needs to be durable and washable. Ideally it should be a natural flooring of stone, slate, terracotta, or quarry tiles, which can then be softened with some form of matting.

Think about safety, too. Use double-glazed panes, which can have insulated blinds sandwiched between the layers, and a double layer of transparent roofing material. Some sunroom roofs are made of glass, in which case it should be special safety or wired glass; some are made of transparent plastic, and again thought should be given to safety, in case of a heavy snowfall, or debris falling onto the roof in bad weather. Laminated glass is recommended for vulnerable areas such as the entrance door.

Building a sunroom obviously changes the shape and dimensions of your home, and this must be considered before taking what is a fairly major step. Feng shui practitioners strongly advise that you consult a feng shui master before possibly unsettling home and fortune with an extra dimension.

Plants provide a healthy environment in which to relax.

If your home is becoming cramped, and you have the space and budget, a sunroom can provide an extra area that is ideal for relaxation.

Take into account the many ways you may want to use your sunroom—as a greenhouse, study, or games room—in order to design the perfect space.

Depending on your taste and budget, you can opt for the cool elegance of a large, formal conservatory or a more simple sunny, plant-filled extension. Both create health-giving links with nature.

LIGHT

Light and life go hand in hand. Nothing is more conducive to a healthy home than good light or lighting. In Scandinavia, for instance, the arrival of snow is greeted with pleasure because the available light increases as it is reflected off the snow. We need clear natural light from the sun to raise our spirits and make us feel good; in fact, research increasingly shows how lack of daylight can cause psychological problems such as depression or seasonal affective disorder (SAD). The creative use of light in our homes can do much to prevent such problems. As natural light changes during the day, it can affect our mood, promoting energetic enthusiasm in the morning and a calmer, more reflective mood in the evening as the sun goes down. The presence of natural light in the home also provides a pleasing link between indoors and out.

So when you are planning your home, you should think about allocating rooms according to the amount of natural light they receive, as well as for other practical reasons. The traditional artists' studio, for example, usually had a large north-facing window, so the painter had as pure and cool a light as possible to avoid distorting colors on the canvas. Morning light is brighter and clearer than afternoon or evening light, which has a more mellow, yellowish cast, so east-facing rooms are cheerful ones to wake up or eat breakfast in. By contrast, a warm evening light will be comfortable and relaxing for a living room.

Obviously, however, as the day wears on, natural light fades and we need to use artificial lighting. There is an enormous range of artificial lighting choices available today, and you need to plan your lighting just as carefully as any other structure or service in your home so it is an integral part of your environment. Thinking about the direction, strength, and type of lighting that you are going to use, and where you are going to put electrical wiring, light fixtures, and sockets, is just as important as thinking about any other decorative feature. The way you use lighting is an essential part of creating a healthy home environment; if you plan wisely, natural and artificial light will complement each other.

Lighting, like color, creates both mood and atmosphere. It has the ability to overwhelm or enhance, dim or brighten any space. Light and color are closely interrelated; the amount of light a color receives can change its appearance subtly, so the two should always be considered together.

INTRODUCING MORE LIGHT

Sunlight streaming through a well-placed stained glass window helps to brighten a dark stairway and throws interesting shadows onto the floor.

THERE IS NO SUBSTITUTE for natural daylight; its very presence encourages health and well-being. Unfortunately, during winter and in northern climates, sunlight can be limited. Low-ceilinged houses with small windows, deep basements, city housing overshadowed by neighboring properties, and suburban or country houses surrounded by trees may also lack sufficient natural light. However, there are many ways of letting more natural light into the house, not only to brighten the home but also to create a greater feeling of space and to reduce reliance on artificial lighting.

Some light-increasing ideas involve structural alterations and building work taking time and often proving to be expensive; others are simpler, more "cosmetic" changes. Keeping rooms streamlined and free of clutter, for instance, encourages a sense of light. Pale colors and shiny textures reflect light, so using a silky-textured wallpaper or vinyl silk latex on walls and/or ceilings will help to brighten a room and create an impression of greater space. Such effects can also be created by using gloss paint on woodwork; polished cotton or silk and satin for curtains; and metals such as brass, chrome, and silver for curtain poles, furniture frames, or accessories. Remember, however, that too many shiny textures in one room can be disturbing and overbright.

Basement apartments are often dark, particularly those overlooked by an exterior wall, which prevents light from penetrating the interior. Painting the outside wall or the area opposite the window in white, pale yellow, or blue can help to reflect more light through the window. Using these colors in the decoration of individual rooms can also help to create a sense of light.

Blinds diffuse direct sunlight, which can cause uncomfortable glare, to create a more muted, softer light. Shiny surfaces such as glass and chrome reflect light and add brightness but can be dazzling.

LIGHT THROUGH GLASS

Glass is another light producer. Glass-topped tables on metal legs will look as if they are floating and help to increase a feeling of spaciousness. Glass shelves placed across a recess, or even across a "blind" window, lit from above or below and perhaps used to display a collection of colored glass or plants, will effectively increase light and reflect any sunlight that does come through the windows.

Stained glass windows or doors also create interesting colored shadows on walls, ceilings, and floors as light shines through them, creating a jewel-like brilliance. Such treatments need to be used with care because too much stained glass or heavy window treatments with small panes can cut natural light and should only be used if they suit the architectural style.

ADAPTING WINDOWS

If you are considering structural changes to your home, you can increase light by replacing existing windows with larger ones, installing energy-saving sealed double- or triple-glazing at the same time. Picture windows and sliding patio doors are particularly effective ways of bringing daylight into the home, but bear in mind the need for harmony with the environment, and the architectural style of your property; such additions can be jarring if they are not in style. You can also create spacious, light areas by knocking down interior walls so light can flood into the home. This sort of dramatic change, however,

59

LIGHT

Curtains should be pulled well back to allow as much light as possible to enter a room.

needs to be planned with considerable care so that you do not cause structural damage to your home.

If structural changes are too drastic, then there is much you can do with your existing windows. Obviously clean windows encourage light in their own right. But you can also let in more light by using curtains or other window treatments creatively. If you are using lined curtains, place the curtain track or pole fairly high above the window and take it well beyond the curtain frame so the curtains can be pulled back clear of the window during the daytime. You can also tie them back or hold them out of the way with wall attachments. Valances at the top of windows can cut light, so make sure they, too, are positioned high up, with the lower edge in line with the top of the window frame. Simple blinds such as slatted Venetian blinds or windowshades

Adding new windows allows more natural light into the home. A well-placed window brightens a bathroom, skylights let light into windowless areas such as attics or landings, and French doors provide a pleasing link with the outdoors.

are less light-restricting and allow you to control the diffusion of daylight into the room.

Fine sheer voile or lace drapes running from floor to ceiling or wall to wall also diffuse light in interesting ways. They can also be used to hide ugly views.

Other ways of increasing a sense of light include using glass bricks as exterior panels in brick walls, or setting glass fish tanks or terrariums into interior walls. These add light, interest, and a feeling of calm. To augment the daylight, consider installing glazed skylights in the roof or on landings, where the extra light will brighten halls. You can also add sloping roof windows. If you want to provide additional sunlit spaces by creating a sunroom or an atrium, bear in mind that an extension can actually cut light or introduce a sense of gloom into the adjoining room.

Light-encouraging tricks

Mirrors are an effective way of increasing light because any reflected light makes a room look larger; glazed pictures and prints can also help. Think carefully about where to position mirrors, perhaps using a helpful partner to judge the effect before committing yourself. You can also do a dummy run with silver foil before hanging the mirror. Remember that a mirror is heavy, so it needs to be mounted firmly with special mirror plates and screws, or screwed to the wall with countersunk screws hidden behind domed metal heads.

Mirrors are also an effective way of magnifying artificial light. Mirrors can be hung in recesses, lit from above with concealed lighting; placed behind a candle flame or oil lamp, which themselves can be put on a sheet of mirror glass, hung in a hall to enhance the effect of a central pendant light or chandelier, or hung above an attractive fireplace. Mirror tiles stuck to a wall also reflect light, but make sure your wall is perfectly smooth or reflections will be distorted. Such tiles can have a sterile look, and are probably best confined to kitchens or hi-tech settings.

Well-positioned mirrors reflect light and bring a feeling of greater space to any room. For best effect, mirrors should be kept clean and sparkling.

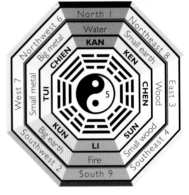

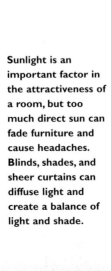

Natural sunlight is energy in its truest form, so light plays an important part in feng shui philosophy. Feng shui recognizes the need for artificial lighting in certain instances, but places greater emphasis on bringing natural light into the home, or using your home in a thoughtful and creative way to make maximum use of natural light during daylight hours, reserving other sources of light, symbolic of the fire element, to enhance, activate, or boost energy levels and lighting when necessary.

In feng shui, sunlight is associated with yang; shade with yin. The aim of feng shui is always to achieve balance and harmony, so when organizing rooms, your aim should be to achieve a balance between the amount of sunlight let into a room and the amount of

shade the room receives. Living areas need healthy and bright amounts of sunlight; well-lit living areas encourage good chi or energy flow. However, too much direct sun can cause headaches and oppressive feelings, which can be counteracted by reducing glare and introducing shade, or by hanging a crystal in the window to break up the sunbeams.

The positioning of your home affects the amount of natural light available, and therefore the way energy flows through the home. South-facing rooms receive full light, ideal if you need more fire energy or want to activate energy levels. East-facing rooms will receive light from the rising sun; west-facing rooms, light from the setting sun. North- or northeast-facing rooms will not receive much

Lighting can be chosen according to the element associated with a particular direction; candles for example, could be used in a south-facing room as that direction is associated with fire.

Sunlight is an important factor in the attractiveness of a room, but too much direct sun can fade furniture and cause headaches. Blinds, shades, and sheer curtains can diffuse light and create a balance of light and shade.

direct light. It is possible to let more daylight into your home by making structural changes, but feng shui practitioners warn that such changes may disrupt the balance of the home and need to be considered carefully. An alternative is to use different rooms according to the way light changes during the day.

LIGHT ENHANCERS

Feng shui has many ways of encouraging light into the home. The use of beautiful colors, light-reflecting textures, and uncluttered space in themselves encourage a sense of lightness. Light-reflecting objects such as crystals or mirrors can be strategically placed to encourage light, boost energy levels, and direct energy around the house. By day, mirrors will reflect natural light; at night, they can maximize light from candles or lamps. Too many mirrors, however, will speed up energy flow, creating hyperactivity and conflict, so they should be used carefully, and should not face each other.

You can also make maximum use of kinetic, or moving, lighting, by installing an open fireplace, using lit candles, especially in the northeast part of the home, which should be used for quiet and contemplation. Candles have a gathering influence and also boost fire energy; placed in water they create a perfect balance between the fire (yang) and water (yin) elements. At night feng shui also advises making use of moonlight to enhance light in the home when the hours of daylight are over.

Moonlight streaming into a room casts a tranquil light over the scene and is an example of good feng shui.

The elements of fire and water are perfectly balanced when lit candles are placed in water.

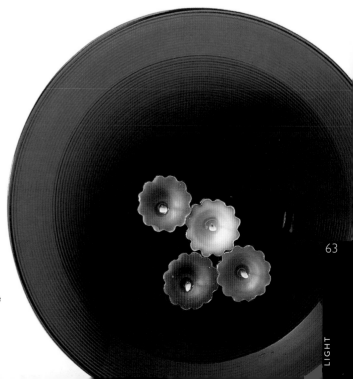

63

TYPES OF LIGHTING

IF WE WERE in complete harmony with our surroundings, we would go to bed when the sun disappears. But this is not the case, and we can increase the hours of lightness, brighten dark areas in the home, and encourage positive feelings by using artificial lighting. This may be harsher and brasher than daylight, but it can be directed, diffused, and reflected in different ways in order to enhance the home, meet specific needs, and create mood.

There are many different types of artificial lighting, which vary according to function, effect, and light source. They also vary according to the type of light fixture. These come in two basic types: structural or architectural, and decorative.

Structural, or architectural, lighting fixtures are part of the basic room design and are often built in unobtrusively. Types of structural lighting include downlighting, spotlighting, wall-washing, uplighting, and concealed strip lighting

Decorative lighting, fixtures, as the name suggests, are not only light sources, but also provide a decorative element. They include table and standard lamps, wall lights, pendants, and chandeliers, and are usually chosen to enhance a room's style and to blend with its color scheme. When choosing lights in this category, always check them during daylight, when light shines onto them, and at night, with light shining through them as their style can change in different conditions.

Artificial lighting falls into three main categories: general or background (top); display or accent (center); and task (right).

Don't try to cope with home wiring yourself. Most electrical installations should be done by professionals to prevent the risk of shock, heat build-up, and possible fire risks.

Spotlight   *Downlight*   *Uplight*   *Strip light*

Lighting is often defined according to function. The main categories are:

General or background lighting, also known as ambient lighting, provides the general lighting for a room, often from a central source.

Accent or display lighting can be used to highlight particular features. Other categories include kinetic or "moving" light such as flickering candles or firelight to provide mood and atmosphere and specialized lighting such as garden or security lights and novelty lights.

Task lighting provides a direct or concentrated source for specific needs such as reading or working in the kitchen.

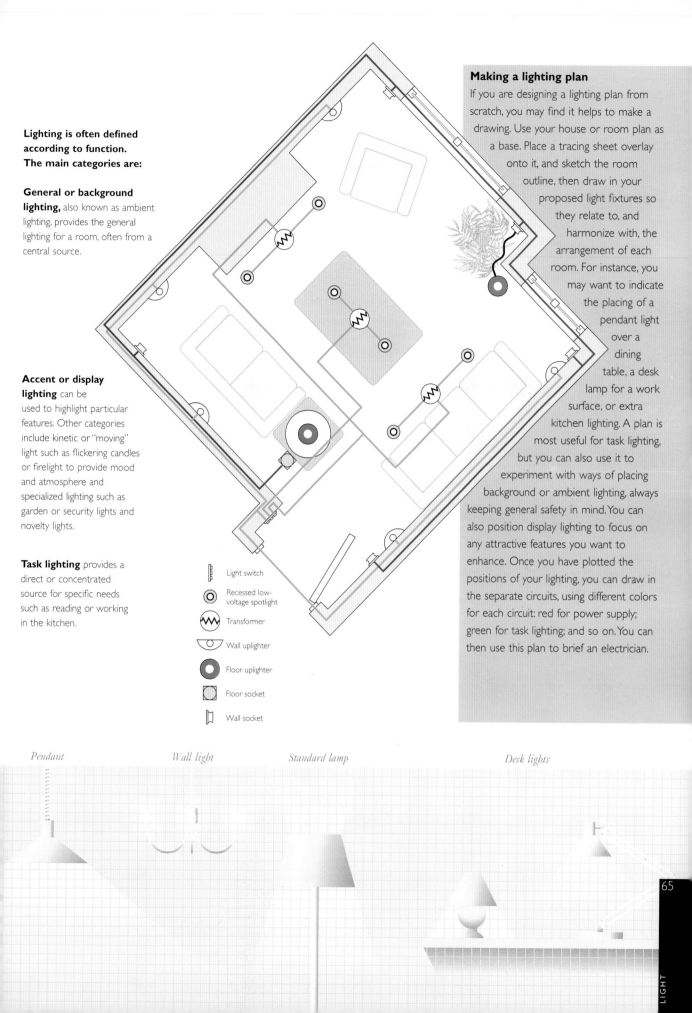

Light switch
Recessed low-voltage spotlight
Transformer
Wall uplighter
Floor uplighter
Floor socket
Wall socket

Making a lighting plan

If you are designing a lighting plan from scratch, you may find it helps to make a drawing. Use your house or room plan as a base. Place a tracing sheet overlay onto it, and sketch the room outline, then draw in your proposed light fixtures so they relate to, and harmonize with, the arrangement of each room. For instance, you may want to indicate the placing of a pendant light over a dining table, a desk lamp for a work surface, or extra kitchen lighting. A plan is most useful for task lighting, but you can also use it to experiment with ways of placing background or ambient lighting, always keeping general safety in mind. You can also position display lighting to focus on any attractive features you want to enhance. Once you have plotted the positions of your lighting, you can draw in the separate circuits, using different colors for each circuit: red for power supply; green for task lighting; and so on. You can then use this plan to brief an electrician.

Pendant   *Wall light*   *Standard lamp*   *Desk lights*

LIGHT
FIXTURES

This pendant lamp eliminates glare by reflecting light back onto the ceiling.

YOUR CHOICE of light fixtures will depend on personal taste, room style and color, how much light you need, where you want to direct it, and what you want the light to do. In practice, most rooms contain a mix of light fixtures. Lamp shades and covers, whether glass, metal, fabric, or other materials, affect the quality of light.

For good feng shui, avoid sharp, angular, or pointed light shapes and fixtures. These cause disharmony and attract hostile energy, because of the "poison arrows" that they create.

PENDANTS AND CHANDELIERS

provide general or background lighting. Usually suspended centrally from the ceiling, they can generate a dull and unflattering light, leaving room corners in darkness. The right lampshade can counteract this negative effect. A wide, conical lampshade reflects light back onto the ceiling; an enclosed shade such as a paper lantern will provide softer lighting and hide the bulb. Some pendants are designed for use over dining tables, when they are best combined with a rise-and-fall mechanism. Direct glare and strong overhead lighting should be avoided; they are very oppressive.

Glass chandeliers are particularly elegant. Originally they were candle-powered and provided a magical light. Converted to electricity, they can be harsh and need low-wattage candle-type bulbs. In feng shui, chandeliers are held to be auspicious and should be placed in the center of the home, where they symbolize the earth element.

Effective lighting can transform a room. Experiment with styles—the broad illumination of halogen lamps, light-diffusing wall elements, directional ceiling fixtures—to achieve the desired effect.

WALL LIGHTS provide a warm, soft background glow and can be decorative. They need to be sited about two-thirds up the height of a wall. This type of light includes uplighters, usually opaque bowl-shaped fixtures that "bounce" light off the ceiling; for feng shui, they can therefore direct energy upward and outward into all the corners of the room. Some uplighters can be used for display lighting, particularly to provide dramatic light from below; a floor-mounted fixture, for instance, could be placed under a glass-topped table to light a selection of plants.

DOWNLIGHTERS are
ceiling-mounted and usually recessed into the ceiling. They project light downward onto a horizontal surface and can be used above dining tables or kitchen surfaces. Several can be used together, possibly with their beams crossed to create a warm, overall glow. They will make a ceiling appear darker and lower. They can be used for background, task, and display lighting.

WALLWASHERS are
another form of downlighter, generally mounted on the ceiling around the perimeter of the room. They effectively "wash" walls with light, giving an impression of pushing a wall outward, so creating a sense of space, useful in a narrow room. Wallwashers can also be used as display lighting for paintings or attractive items of furniture, or for task lighting.

BUILT-IN INDIRECT LIGHTING provides a com-
fortable background glow and can also be combined with different architectural features such as molding. It can be positioned above wall-mounted cabinets to throw light onto the ceiling, or inside display cabinets.

Spotlights are often used for task lighting, because they are directional. There are "eyeball" spotlights, which are often recessed, as well as bracket-mounted and wall spotlights. Most can be angled so that the light shines in a specific direction. They can also be combined with a special lighting track, usually ceiling-mounted but possibly wall- or floor-mounted. Spotlights are particularly effective in small kitchens where there are several surfaces that need clear light. They can also be used as display lighting to illuminate pictures.

TABLE, DESK, AND STANDARD LAMPS are
most frequently used as task lighting, placed where they are needed to provide a constant, direct, and clear stream of light.

Table and standard lamps can also be used for general background glow, and as decorative lighting to enhance a color scheme or to introduce contrast.

SHADED FLUORESCENTS are an
alternative for task-lighting requirements, placed over a workbench in a hobbies area, under top cupboards to light a work surface below, or to illuminate shelves.

LIGHT SOURCES

Thomas Edison
(1847–1931) the **US**
scientist who
invented the electric
light bulb in 1879,
leading to the
development of a
wide range of
lighting options in
the home.

The balance of light
from a variety of
sources and
directions—glass
doors, high windows
or skylights,
recessed
downlighting,
reflected light from
the walls—creates
an inviting ambience
in harmony with
feng shui principles.

NIGHTTIME LIGHTING is much more dependent on the development of technology than any other area of interior design, and for centuries not a lot happened. It is only in the last few decades that home lighting has become more adventurous, taking inspiration from display and stage lighting so that low-voltage and other modern lighting techniques have become feasible for use in the home.

Originally an orange glow from firelight or rush lights, primitive oil lamps, and candles was the only means of extending daylight beyond dusk, with the light source sometimes magnified by metal or a mirror placed behind it. In some grand 18th-century rooms, window shutters were backed with mirror glass, reflecting the glittering light from chandeliers and creating the impression of light still shining through the windows.

In 1780 the Argand oil lamp was invented, with a capillary-action controllable wick that made it possible to adjust the light level, which transformed home lighting. Gas lighting was developed in the 1850s, first for street lighting, and later for home use. Both inventions brought about enormous social change. By the 1880s, electricity was beginning to supersede gas; it needed an incandescent tungsten-filament electric light bulb to supply the light source.

From those early beginnings has developed a wide range of artificial light sources to be used in the home.

INCANDESCENT

INCANDESCENT light is used for much domestic lighting. It has a slightly yellowish cast, gives a warm light, and will provide a "slice" of uniform light, although the amount of light will depend on wattage and fixture.

TUNGSTEN

TUNGSTEN The original incandescent tungsten-filament light bulb gave off a harsh crude, white light that was not restful to the eye. Tungsten filament can also supply a reddish light with a fairly long life; the brighter white light bulb was much more short-lived. Compromise was reached with a bulb that gives off a slightly yellow cast and is still used today in most home light fixtures. It tends to make reds, pinks, tans, yellows, and neutrals look warmer, but to dull down greens and blues. "Pearlizing" the bulb can soften the light slightly; silvering it will create a clearer light; colored bulbs can distort light—and color schemes —but are useful for creating a specific mood.

TUNGSTEN HALOGEN INCANDESCENT

TUNGSTEN HALOGEN INCANDESCENT lamps have been developed more recently. The filament in the center of the bulb is surrounded by halogen gas, which gives a brighter, whiter light and up to 40 percent more light than the equivalent tungsten-filament incandescent bulb. It also has longer life—up to 2,000 hours. These lamps are used mainly in spotlights and uplights, and for garden and security lighting. Halogen lights must be used with care as they produce a great deal of heat; when used indoors they are best combined with a dimmer switch to control the light level.

FLUORESCENT

FLUORESCENT lighting provides a flat, cool light that casts few shadows and creates no highlights. Fluorescent lights were long considered unsuitable for most home-lighting purposes, as the light they gave off was considered cold and unflattering. Now, however, various different-color tubes are available, which give a slightly warmer, pinker light. They are long-lasting and energy-saving, and some have been adapted into bulb or circular shapes to fit wall lights and table or standard lights, which would normally take only incandescent lights. They tend to give off a harsh light and an annoying buzzing. They can cause headaches and eyestrain, and it can be stressful to sit in a room where they are used. Feng shui would advise against their use altogether.

LOW-VOLTAGE

LOW-VOLTAGE lighting is most successful when used to provide accent and display lighting, because it gives a clear and direct light, as well as good color rendition. The tightly-controlled narrow beam can be used to create a dramatic effect; the fixtures are discreet and the light is safe and cool to the touch. It is also more economical to run than main-voltage lighting, although the initial outlay will be more expensive. Low-voltage lighting comes in many forms from downlighters and wallwashers to lamps and uplighters. It is not suitable for general lighting, because of the narrow beam of light that it gives off—but double-focus downlighters, or masses of tiny "starlights" can be used to provide adequate background lighting.

FULL-SPECTRUM

FULL-SPECTRUM lighting comes in incandescent bulbs and fluorescent tubes, and has been designed to reproduce daylight. Some consider it to be mood-enhancing and beneficial for those who suffer in the absence of sun.

Overcoming SAD

Research shows that moods and behavior can vary according to season, apparently in response to differing light levels. The most striking effects occur in people who suffer from seasonal affective disorder (SAD), who, every fall and winter, may experience depression, apathy, and tiredness. The mechanisms causing SAD are not yet understood, but exposure to bright full-spectrum lamps and special daytime lighting can alleviate symptoms.

ASSESSING NEEDS

MOST ROOMS in the healthy home will use several different types of light: general background lighting; task lighting; accent and display. But how much do you need?

Comfortable light levels are a matter of personal preference. Safety and health are obviously priorities, and you will need to light dark corners, changes in floor level, and flights of stairs, provide adequate task lighting to avoid eyestrain. Fairly bright home lighting was once the norm and is still preferred by many, but the current emphasis is on energy conservation, and the trend is toward clear, defined light for working areas, with any surrounding areas more softly lit.

There is also a trend toward greater flexibility in the way rooms are used in the home. A general-purpose living room, for example, needs clear lighting over the dining area while food is being eaten, with the sitting area dimmed to a soft background glow. When the meal is over, the dining area lights can be switched off or dimmed, and the lighting in the sitting area can be turned up.

When you are planning how much light is needed for a given activity and area, consider the intricacy of the task to be performed. Close work such as sewing, bookkeeping, model-making, and so on will require a lot of light. Think, too, about the color of the working surfaces; darker materials, and those with little color contrast, need a higher level of light than black writing on white paper. The eyesight of the person engaged in the task is also important—older people may need more light than those with younger eyes.

Adjusting lighting between one area of a general-purpose room and another helps to define areas. Here the dining table (far left) is lit from overhead when in use, while more general lighting levels are switched on when the sitting area is in use (left).

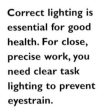

Correct lighting is essential for good health. For close, precise work, you need clear task lighting to prevent eyestrain.

It is also important to avoid glare; too much light coming off a bright, white, or shiny surface will tend to contribute to eyestrain. It is also essential to light computer and television screens carefully. Reflected light "bouncing back" can be distracting. It is often better to place a lamp behind or at the side of a television set, and to light a computer keyboard but not the screen.

LIGHT MEASUREMENT
When measuring light levels, it is usual to consider the light coming from a given source, or bulb. The luminous intensity of a light source is expressed in candelas (one candela is approximately equal to the luminous intensity of one dinner candle); the amount of light energy flowing from that source is expressed in lumens. You can roughly estimate the lumen level of any room by totaling the lumens emitted from all the bulbs illuminating that room. For instance, one candle produces about 12 lumens; a 60-watt incandescent bulb produces about 1,000 lumens (17 lumens per watt), and an 80-watt high-efficiency fluorescent tube produces 4,500 lumens (57 lumens per watt). You will find figures on the packaging of all bulbs.

You can then relate these measurements to your specific needs. As a rough guide, you need a minimum of 2,500 lumens for intricate visual tasks, directed at the work surface. Casual task and general background lighting require about 1,500 to 2,000 lumens, with lighting arranged comfortably.

Color temperature chart measured in degrees Kelvin.

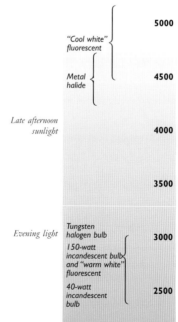

9000 *Degrees Kelvin*

General light from blue sky—not sunlight 8500

8000

7500

Overcast sky 7000

6500

6000

Direct summer sunlight overhead at midday 5500

5000

"Cool white" fluorescent

Metal halide 4500

Late afternoon sunlight 4000

3500

Evening light Tungsten halogen bulb 3000

150-watt incandescent bulb and "warm white" fluorescent

40-watt incandescent bulb 2500

2000

1500

The coolness or warmth of light is something else to consider when you are planning your lighting. Natural daylight is the usual point of reference, but some daylight can appear very cool. The light from a blue or overcast sky, for instance, or from a northerly direction is usually much cooler or bluer than the clearer, purer white sunlight overhead at midday.

You can use a Kelvin chart to assess the degree of warmth or coolness of any form of light, both natural and artificial. The scale is given in terms of degrees Kelvin, which defines the "color temperature" of a given light, from blue, through white, yellow, orange, and red. Artificial light ranges from 5,000 degrees—cool white fluorescence—through the warmer fluorescents, low-voltage and metal halide lighting, tungsten halogen, then the incandescent bulb. Two of the warmest non-bulb-generated lights are the light of a flickering candle and the kinetic light of a glowing fire.

Fire can produce a wonderful flickering light, ideal for relaxation and thinking, but not suitable for close work such as reading.

LIGHTING ROOM BY ROOM

Wall sconces give dramatic, diffused light, while overhead lamps clearly illuminate the stairs and entrance for safety.

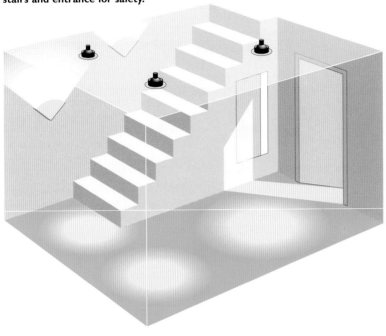

HALLS, STAIRS, AND LANDINGS
These areas need to be brightly lit, both for safety and to create a welcoming atmosphere. Stairs must be well lit so the treads can be seen clearly; a dual switch linking the hall and landing is advisable. The landing light could be on a dimmer switch so that a soft light can be kept on for young children. Table, desks, or telephone areas should have separately switched task lighting.

Use wallwashers to focus any architectural features or wall hangings. If the hall is long and narrow, use mirrors to reflect light; hang an eye-catching item on a narrow wall and light it dramatically.

LIVING AREAS
These may be split-function areas. If so, the individual areas will need appropriate lighting according to their different function.

Provide soft general background lighting, possibly using a dimmer switch. Use task lighting for reading and games areas, or for any desk area. Light shelves or display cabinets, possibly using built-in light. Use accent or display lighting to enhance interesting architectural features.

If one of your rooms doubles as a living space and spare bedroom, make sure that table lamps can be plugged in conveniently as bedside lighting.

DINING ROOM
Provide a soft, background glow, perhaps with built-in lighting. Light the dining table clearly, but avoid any glare. You may choose overhead

General background lighting with the focus of a pendant lamp over the table gives suitable coverage for a dining room. Remember that a stationary pendant lamp can make rearranging the furniture problematic.

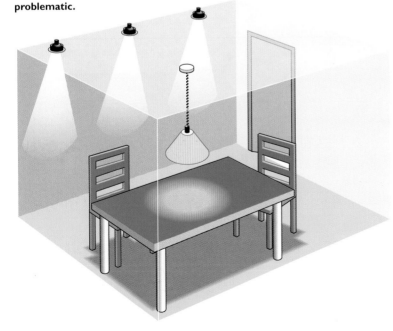

lighting, perhaps a pendant that can be raised or lowered according to what is required. Feng shui warns against using a powerful overhead light as it throws too powerful an energy force onto diners. Candlelight on a dining table provides both light and a pleasant atmosphere that leads to harmonious socializing.

Food serving areas should be well lit, perhaps with wall lights or lamps that can be switched off or dimmed once the meal is in progress. Use spotlights to focus architectural features, paintings, or beautiful objects.

Be sure to provide appropriate task lighting if part of the room is also used as a study.

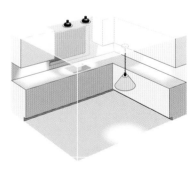

KITCHENS This is the main "workroom" of the home. It needs good task lighting, some soft background lighting, and perhaps some accent and display lighting focused on a hutch. Clear, direct lighting is extremely important. Work surfaces and stoves should be well lit from above. Sinks are often placed under a window and receive good natural light during the day; at night, they too will need an extra light source.

Eating areas in the kitchen will need to be well lit, and you can install built-in lighting in deep storage cupboards. Outlets will need to be seen easily at night.

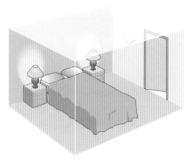

BEDROOMS The type of lighting will be influenced by the way the room is used. You may need to place nightlighting in a child's bedroom and task lighting in a room used by a teenager. Bedrooms also need soft, background lighting, best controlled from door and bed. Feng shui experts would strongly advise against placing ceiling lights such as pendant lights directly over the head of the bed, as they will disturb energy.

Bedside lighting can be wall-mounted or built into the bedhead, but should be directed to light the pages of a book when someone is reading in bed. Feng shui recommends the use of side lights for reading rather than downlights, as light pouring onto readers' heads can be disturbing.

Any dressing table area will need good task lighting.

If television is watched in bed, or there is a computer in the room, avoid any light that will cause glare from the screen.

BATHROOMS Water and electricity do not mix, so safety is of prime importance. Lights can be switched by a pull-cord system, or switches can be placed outside the bathroom door; fixtures should be covered with glass or plastic so metal parts are unaffected by steam. Many spotlights, uplighters, and downlighters are therefore unsuitable for a bathroom. Light any mirror/dressing table area with a clear light that shines onto the face and not the mirror.

Light bathtub, basin, and shower areas well but not too brightly; shiny surfaces can give off glare. Showers need special sealed fixtures.

The bathroom is an ideal setting for kinetic (moving) lighting in the form of candles or oil lamps. For pure relaxation at the end of the day, you can soak in a bath surrounded by flickering candles.

PLAY AND GAMES ROOMS These rooms need good background lighting plus some accent or display lighting. Task lighting, however, will be the most important lighting feature and will depend entirely on how the room is being used.

Desks and play and games surfaces need to be well and separately lit; billiard, ping pong, and pool tables need special table lighting.

Safety point

If using candles or oil lamps, make sure they are placed safely and securely. Be sure to extinguish them before leaving the room or area.

SUNROOMS AND GARDENS

Light fixtures can add hours of use to your sunroom by making it attractive after dark. Choose low-voltage or hydroponic lighting to assist plant growth, or opt for the natural light of candles.

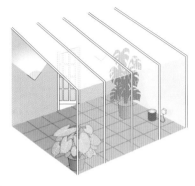

As outdoor lighting gains in popularity, the variety of fixtures increases. Movable lights on spikes and ground-level spotlights can highlight foliage or give added security.

SUNROOMS People often neglect artificial lighting for conservatories because these rooms receive plenty of natural daylight. After dark, use uplighters for good background lighting, concealed behind or inside plant pots. Also provide adequate lighting for dining and sitting areas. Lighting doesn't need to be electric; the soft glow or flickering flames of candles and oil lamps looks wonderful, but do remember to extinguish the flame before you leave. You can use special hydroponic lighting to encourage plant growth and uplighters or spotlights to illuminate particular plants. Low-voltage lighting is particularly good because it does not become too hot. Make sure that no lights are placed so close to foliage that they might scorch the plants or even cause a fire.

GARDEN or outdoor lighting is an increasingly popular type of lighting design. It can be used to emphasize plants, to enhance architectural or water features, and to create a closer link between your home and your garden. As outdoor entertaining becomes more popular, after-dark lighting also serves a practical purpose.

The golden rule when planning outdoor lighting, however, is that a little light goes a long way; it is essential to plan lighting so that it does not dazzle either yourself or others. Ideally, try to plan the lighting at the same time as you plan the garden. At night a 20-watt lamp—even 12 watts—can seem very bright. And a backyard, however pretty, should be lit with discretion and subtlety if it is not to resemble a football stadium.

As with indoor lighting, fixtures and degree of light need to be chosen according to function, whether the aim is security, decoration, task lighting, or the creation of mood.

Your front door and entrance should be well lit, as should any front path, steps, or changes in level. Outdoor cooking areas also need appropriate lighting. You may also need to supply garages and garden sheds with light and power so that you can use them effectively at night. This may involve running cables from the main power supply; these should be covered or buried well underground. Any light fixtures you use should also be specifically made for outdoor use, with all their metal and electrical parts fitted with antiglare cowls and louvers to reduce glare.

Some garden lights are low-voltage and can be tucked away discreetly; others are on spikes, which makes them very flexible. You can move them to highlight different plants throughout the year, or to focus on specific areas within the garden.

Candles, lanterns, and oil lamps are portable and provide beautiful, natural light indoors or out. Be sure to extinguish them when you leave the area.

Use light to enhance attractive outdoor features such as a gazebo, old wall, garden pond, fountain, or outdoor statues. You can also use light to accentuate plants rambling up walls, or trailing down from balconies—white flowers with good green foliage are particularly effective when lit this way. Many climbing plants, such as jasmine or honeysuckle, are scented, and so bring extra pleasure to the senses.

You can light these features with spotlights or with downlights, provided you have somewhere to place the fixtures, such as under the house eaves, in the "roof" of a gazebo or arbor, or even attached to tree branches. For a softer effect you can use diffused lighting mounted onto house or garden walls. Sometimes throwing a tree or other feature into sharp silhouette is even more dramatic and effective; you can achieve this effect by using a spotlight aimed at the fence or wall from close behind the plant.

Strings of lights, too, either decorative minilights such as those used for outdoor decorating or even strings of colored lights, can all look magical in the yard strung between trees or over a trellis. They also light a dining area subtly if there are enough trees from which to hang them, or if the area has its own arbor or awning to contain the light.

But not all outdoor lighting has to be electrical. Kinetic lighting can be very effective and

Safety point

Make sure any changes of level in the garden are well lit to avoid accidents. Garden and sunroom light fixtures and electrical cables must be designed for outdoor use; fixtures must be kept moisture-free.

creates fascinating plays of light. Candles, oil lamps, or hurricane lamps can be placed on tables and walls or can even be wall-mounted to wonderful effect. Garden flares, usually on long spikes, can be pushed into the earth.

Swimming pools and water features should always be carefully lit, because of the potential danger of electricity combined with water. Security lighting is usually controlled with a sensor, which comes on as a person approaches, but some are so sensitive they are set off too easily, causing annoyance and light pollution. An alternative is timed security lighting that can be sited near the front and back doors, or near a garage.

All artificial outdoor lighting should be controlled from inside the house; in some cases, however, you may want to install dual switches, so you can dim the lights when you are outside.

One of the earliest forms of artificial lighting, candles produce a wonderful kinetic light that, in feng shui, is considered to produce a "gathering" energy, drawing people to the light source.

COLOR

Life without color, with everything seen in monochrome, is inconceivable. Imagine a world that did not contain multi-colored rainbows, dramatic sunsets, or the brilliant colors of plants and insects. Color affects us emotionally, physically and spiritually. Color stimulates our senses, encouraging us to relax or be active. Colors can make us feel hot or cold, happy or sad. Some can even induce an appetite for food.

Color, well-being, and emotions are closely linked, and our reactions to color are often deep and intuitive. Color affects not only how a room looks, but also how it feels. Think of how you might feel in an all-black bedroom, then imagine how different you would feel in an all-yellow room. The colors you choose to decorate your home will reflect you as a person, your personality and outlook. They will also help you to create a specific mood, ambience, or atmosphere in which you can relax, work, or entertain. Colors can also play eye-deceiving tricks, making a large room seem smaller and cozier, or a small room calm and more spacious. You can use color to focus attention on good features and disguise or camouflage less attractive ones.

For these reasons, color is one of the most important aspects of your home, yet in itself it costs very little. It is no more expensive to create a particular scheme that is stimulating and exciting, or calming and relaxing, than to choose color randomly, which may result in an overall negative effect, making you feel uncomfortable, depressed, or ill at ease.

DYES AND PIGMENTS

Paint pigments today allow for a greater degree of accuracy in paint mixing than could be achieved with natural sources.

Greek columns

Murex shell

Dyes and pigments came originally from natural sources. Imperial purple came from the crushed fragments of the murex whelk (above); woad leaves produced blue (right). Over time, however, dyes produced from these sources, and used to decorate architectural features, have faded (above, top).

Woad

The colors we use for decoration or interior design are usually created by using pigments, dyes, and glazes—the basic ingredients that give a surface its color. Originally, these could only be obtained from natural sources—plants, minerals, the earth, animals, and insects—which were ground up and suspended in a suitable medium such as oil, animal fat, or a solvent.

The famous Tyrian purple, the color used for the Roman emperor's toga, came from a shellfish, the murex whelk, which, when crushed, gave up a drop of whitish liquid that was used to saturate the cloth; when the liquid dried in sunlight, it turned a deep reddish-purple. Indigo, too, was the result of a color change. Made from wood ash, leaves, and urine, it appeared pale yellow until exposed to the sun.

Early pigments and dyes were not colorfast, and faded or grayed over time. The drab colors we see today in many stately homes or historic buildings give quite the wrong impression of the original architect's or designer's intentions. Scottish architect Robert Adam, for example, used strong jades and magentas; Sir John Soane combined rich Indian reds with strong sulfur yellow; and the ancient Egyptians, Romans, and Greeks used bright, bold color combinations. But when we look at their work today, after centuries of exposure to the elements, we see a pale imitation of the original.

Some past "recipes" for specific colors contained highly toxic ingredients. For example, a particularly striking green used in fabric and wallpaper which was popular during the late 18th and early 19th centuries contained arsenic; as a result, many fabric dyers and wallpaper hangers

who were exposed to this toxic substance became ill, and some even died as a result.

Lead-based paints are also a serious health hazard. Although lead is no longer used to manufacture paint, it is still present in many buildings built before 1980, and home decorators should exercise extreme care when remodeling such homes.

As manufacturing processes improved, ready-mixed paints were developed (paints were, in the past, mixed by decorators on site), machine-woven fabrics became widely available, and wallpapers were printed by roller instead of being hand-blocked. The pigments and dyes used also improved, but they were still not necessarily colorfast.

Modern technology, has made it possible to re-create the brilliant colors that were used in the past. Slivers of paint, small scraps of wallpaper, and tiny threads of fabric can be put under a microscope and analyzed, allowing chemists to reproduce the color accurately.

Modern science has also helped to develop safe, sophisticated coloring and dyeing methods. It is estimated that more than three million dyes and pigments have now been created, many of them from petroleum products. Chemists have experimented with paints, stains, and glazes, and have produced dyes that can be bonded successfully to artificial fibers, allowing an unprecedented variety of colors, which have influenced the fashion scene and interior decorating trends which now change on a regular basis.

Unfortunately, most paints available today, having nonrenewable origins, can themselves have a negative impact on the environment. To balance this, you can also make use of natural materials in the home, such as brick, stone, wood, and textiles, to introduce color to your home.

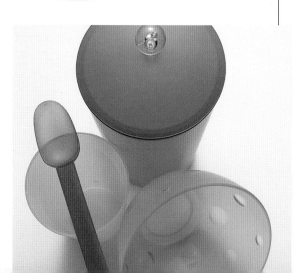

Developments in the chemical industry have produced an enormous range of dyes and coloring processes, resulting in an unprecedented choice of colored paints (far left), fabrics (center left) and even plastics (left).

THE COLOR WHEEL

Rainbow

THE COLOR WHEEL, or color spectrum, is one of the basic tools that we use to analyze and select color. Sir Isaac Newton devised the first color wheel in the 17th century, following his experiments with splitting light, when he discovered the visible spectrum, showing how sunlight breaks down into bands of different wavelengths—the seven colors of the rainbow. Since then, there have been other wheels, such as that developed by Johannes Itten of the Bauhaus, but all show the relationship between different colors.

On the wheel colors are arranged with analogous, or adjacent, colors next to each other, and complementary, or contrasting, colors opposite one another. When arranged in the correct sequence, they form a circle.

Pure colors, also known as hues, make up the twelve colors of the basic wheel including primary, secondary, and tertiary colors. They can have white added to them to lighten their value and

create a pastel; gray added to form a middle tone; or black added to deepen, enrich them, and to make a shade.

Red, yellow, and blue are the primary colors and are equidistant from each other on the wheel. These are the pure, original hues, and they cannot be made by mixing together other colors. But when two primary colors are mixed, they create the secondary colors: blue and red produce violet; blue and yellow produce green; red and yellow produce orange.

When a primary color is mixed in equal parts with the secondary color next to it, the tertiary, or intermediate, colors result: blue/violet, red/violet, red/orange, yellow/orange, yellow/green, and blue/green.

The complete wheel of 12 colors is therefore composed of: blue, blue/violet, violet, red/violet, red, red/orange, orange, yellow/orange, yellow, yellow/green, green, blue/green—and back again to blue.

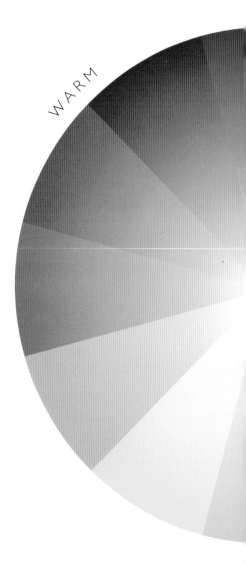

WARM

Color can change the feel of a room dramatically, so use it according to need. Orange is one of the warm colors and can be vibrant and exciting; green, by contrast, is cool, fresh, and elegant.

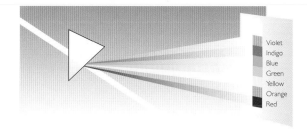

Violet
Indigo
Blue
Green
Yellow
Orange
Red

When white light hits a prism, it separates into the different colors of the spectrum, or rainbow, from red to violet.

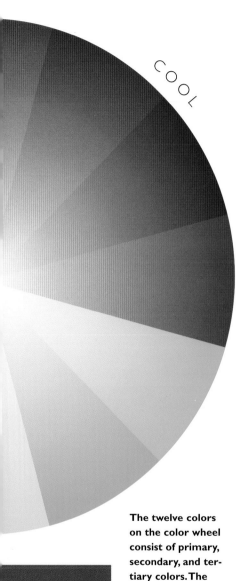

COOL

The twelve colors on the color wheel consist of primary, secondary, and tertiary colors. The sequence in which they appear on the wheel clearly shows the natural division between the warm and cool colors.

WARM AND COOL

The wheel divides down the middle with warm or so-called advancing colors on one side. These are the long-wavelength colors such as red/violet, red, red/orange, orange, yellow/orange, and yellow, which seem to advance or come toward you. Their various tints, tones, and shades are also warm—for example, pink, deep rose, and rich burgundy are all values of red and are warm. Apricot, peach, and terracotta relate back to orange, whereas gold, lemon, and primrose all relate back to yellow; they are all on the warm half of the circle.

The cool or so-called receding colors are to be found on the opposite side of the spectrum. These are the short-wavelength colors such as violet, blue/violet, blue, blue/green, green, and yellow/green. When you look at them, these colors appear to recede or go away from you. Their various values—lilac, mauve, and lavender, for example—are all found on the cool half of the color wheel.

Where the two halves of the wheel join on the cusp, on yellow/green and red/violet, colors may be warm or cool, depending on how much of their adjacent color they contain. For example, some violets are cool when they are mixed with blue, yet are warm when they go toward the red/violet section. Yellow/greens can be warm if a lot of yellow has been used to mix them, or cooler when there is more green.

Understanding color

Four characteristics quantify color: hue, which is the pure color seen on the color wheel; intensity (chroma or saturation), which is the color's relative brightness or dullness; temperature (warmth or coolness); and value (lightness or darkness). Changes of value are created by adding white, gray, or black to the pure color.

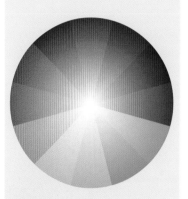

The neutrals

Black, white, and gray are, strictly speaking, noncolors, or neutrals. In their pure form, they are added to the different colors on the color wheel to change the value of a color. Tints are created by adding white; tones by adding gray; or shades by adding black.

In the home, you can use neutrals alone or together to make a neutral scheme, or individually to create contrast or emphasize a color scheme.

COLOR PHILOSOPHY

COLOR PHILOSOPHY is an important feature of feng shui and is closely linked to The Theory of the Five Elements, or energies: Wood, Metal, Fire, Water, and Earth. Each of the elements has its own color. Wood is associated with green, metal with white, fire with red, water with blue or black, and earth with yellow. Each of the colors, like each of the elements, has specific qualities, or fosters certain qualities of life, personality, and health. According to the principles of Chinese philosophy, each person is born into one of the five elements, noted in Chinese calendars, so everyone is influenced by one or other of the elements; and the colors they choose, often intuitively, reflect this situation.

Good feng shui strives to achieve balance and harmony, and color plays a major part in this process, aiming to support, boost, or move the elemental flow of energy throughout the home.

But unlike conventional interior design, feng shui does not follow specific color rules. Feng shui practitioners do not automatically recommend that a particular room should be a particular color. Instead choice of color reflects a person's birth element and therefore personal needs. For instance, people born into the fire element may need to bring more red into their homes to match their energy levels; while people born into the wood element may favor touches of green. Given the way in

which the five elements act on each other, people born into one element may need to be careful when using colors associated with another element.

Individual colors also have symbolic significance, and feng shui practitioners may suggest using colors that are associated with particular goals. The color black, for instance, signifies business success; red promotes luck, growth, or happiness; pink can be a healing color. Association with a desirable attribute, however, does not mean that the color should be used excessively. Sometimes just a touch—perhaps in the form of flowers, or accessories—may be enough to boost energy or bring that element into the home.

WATER WOOD FIRE METAL EARTH

The five elements interact creatively or destructively. In this creative cycle, each element supports or boosts the next. Colors used in this balanced way will promote health and harmony.

METAL

WOOD

EARTH

WATER

FIRE

Here the cycle is destructive. Colors used like this, for instance by putting too much blue (water) into a red (fire) environment will create chaos and ill health.

COLOR
AND
LIGHT

We see color everywhere in the natural world—the changing hues of the sky from the blue of noon to the reds and purples of sunset, or of vegetation from the fresh greens of spring to the vivid russets of fall. But color is simply how our brain perceives different wavelengths of light hitting the eye's retina.

How we see any surface is influenced by light as well as by the pigments, dyes, or glazes used to color it. These compounds absorb light of particular wavelengths efficiently and selectively. The wavelengths that are reflected back determine the specific color we see. Colors themselves are not physical properties but sensations that result from light of different wavelengths reaching the eye, which sees an object only by the light it reflects. Red is the longest wavelength that we can see, blue and violet the shortest. Some objects reflect and absorb light of different wavelengths equally well: black velvet absorbs nearly all the light which falls on it, reflecting only about 5 percent back, so it

appears dark and dull; clean snow reflects nearly all light that falls on it, so it looks white and shiny.

This can also be explained in the terms of a glowing red sunset. At the end of the day, as twilight falls, the changing color of the sky is caused by the changing angle between the sun and earth. As the earth turns eastward, and the sun sinks below the horizon, its rays travel further through the atmosphere to reach us. Since there is more atmosphere to travel through, there are more particles to scatter the light. Shorter wavelengths, such as blue, are filtered out, leaving the longer red or orange wavelengths. The same effect is sometimes created at dawn as the sun rises in the east, but it is never as rich a red as in the evening.

The same principles apply in the home. If an item is lit by a pure white light or seen in daylight, then the color will be more or less pure. But, if the light source is yellowish, bluish, or greenish, it appears to alter the color. As a result, the same object looks quite different when hit by different light sources. A red cushion, for instance, appears red in daylight or when lit by a red light because it reflects only red light and absorbs all the other colors. At night, or when lit

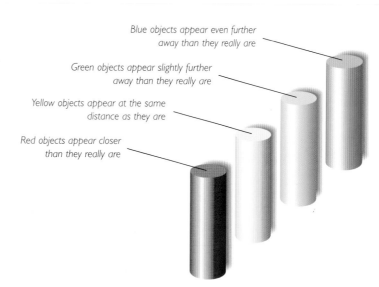

Blue objects appear even further away than they really are

Green objects appear slightly further away than they really are

Yellow objects appear at the same distance as they are

Red objects appear closer than they really are

by a blue light, the same object will look much darker, even black. You should always check materials under the exact lighting conditions where they will be used, because they will look very different in daylight and at night.

Short- and long-wavelength colors

Different colors can look slightly closer or further away than they really are—perhaps because of the way each color is focused on the eye's retina.

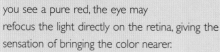

Red light is naturally focused at a point behind the retina when there is a mixture of colors. When you see a pure red, the eye may refocus the light directly on the retina, giving the sensation of bringing the color nearer.

Yellow light is the color we see as brightest. It is focused directly on the retina, and so appears neither to advance like red nor recede like blue.

Blue light is naturally focused at a point in front of the retina when there is a mixture of colors. When you see a pure blue, the eye may refocus the light directly on the retina, giving the sensation of pushing the color further away.

Color vision depends on the millions of light-sensitive cells that line the retina, the back of the eye, and send signals to the brain whenever they are hit by light rays. There are actually two kinds of cell: rods and cones. The rods only react to light and shade and are sensitive even to very dim light. It is the cones that tell you what color light is. Cones are less sensitive, which is why your color vision goes in dim light. Some scientists believe that there are three different kinds of cone, each sensitive to one of the three primary colors. The color we see depends on how much each is stimulated. An alternative view is that there are cones that detect the balance between red and green light or yellow and blue light.

It is easy to see the effect of texture on color by comparing these widely different materials of matching cobalt blue.

Bright daylight shows up the different textures in a room of simple color palette—predominantly dark blue and white. The interest and variety are created by the juxtaposition of coarse with smooth, glossy with matte, silky with basket-weave. The color and texture of straw and sponge provide a natural complement.

COLOR AND TEXTURE

SURFACE TEXTURES can also affect the way we perceive color—many textures reflect light; some absorb it; others filter and diffuse light. Consequently, the same color, created by identical "ingredients" in either the pigment or dye, can appear quite different, depending on the way the surface reacts to the light. You can use this to good effect in the home, incorporating textures into your color schemes and using them to create mood. It is also another reason why you need to look at fabrics, paint, and other color samples under the lighting conditions in which they will actually be used.

Many people think of texture purely as a raised, rough, or sculpted surface, but these are heavily textured materials. All surfaces have a texture, even if it is perfectly smooth and bland, such as flat, plastered walls that have been painted with flat-finish latex. This sort of texture tends to absorb light slightly, making the color look a little weaker or more subtle. The same color on a shiny, reflective surface, such as gloss paint, silk fabric, or glazed tiles, will look brighter and stronger as the light is bounced back.

ROUGH TEXTURES

The rough and rustic textures of exposed brick or stone walls, hefty planks of wood, natural floor coverings, and coarsely woven textiles absorb light, and so make the color appear darker, richer, or in some cases duller. Light-diffusing textures, such as sheer gauze and voile fabrics, allow the light to pass through them, making the color appear softer, more delicate, and more subtle.

Because of their uneven surface, heavily textured items can create very interesting effects. Light is reflected, absorbed, and deflected differently across them, from different parts of such objects, resulting in a kind of "shadow play." The overall effect is one of varied value patterns. You can use this effect in a room where you want to add an extra visual element or dimension, but do not want to feature a bold design.

All materials have texture—even if they are perfectly smooth.

Terracotta tiles provide a rich, earthy base for a room.

The pattern of knotty wood gives visual interest while remaining in the background. The uneven visual image contrasts with the wood's smooth texture.

Fabric is a source of unending variety of texture, from rough-weave linen to the tightest weave of shiny satin to the loopy thickness of terrycloth.

A richly textured fern conjures up the style of a period room, rather than the sleek lines of modern design.

Heavy velvets, brocades, and silks give a sumptuous, period feel to a room. Textures, like colors, can be dominant and overpowering or light and soft, creating different atmospheres and moods.

TEXTURE, like color, can work to bring surfaces forward or give the impression that they are farther away. For example, the shiny and silky textures—glass, brass, chrome, satin, moiré—seem to come toward you; the rougher, soft, and light-absorbing textures—velvet, tweed, and jute—do the reverse and seem to fade into the distance. As a result, the color of a highly glazed ceramic tile stands out much more than the same color on a bath towel.

SETTING A STYLE

Texture can also help to set the style of a room. Some textures, for example, are definitely more traditional, and more suited to period room settings, than others. Brass, gilt, velvet, brocades, limewashed walls, weathered beams, sumptuous silks, lace, and feathery ferns, for example, all have a period feel, while chrome, especially if combined with smoked glass, brushed aluminum, black ash, burlap, gloss-painted metal, and slatted Venetian blinds, all have a more modern image. Some textures, however, such as leather, sheer fabrics, brick, and stone, are timeless; it is the

When you have worked out a design scheme and you find it lacks texture, or for that matter tonal or color contrast, you can add color and contrast by introducing so-called accents: accessories, or multicolored items such as pillows, wall hangings, pictures, rugs, or ornaments.

To judge different textures, you
need to consider the overall effect
the surface will create, and use as
large a sample as possible when
doing your color matching.

way they are used that creates a specific look.

It is very important to achieve textural balance when selecting materials. This means choosing a variety of different textures within the scheme, which will complement and contrast with each other while at the same time relating to the overall style.

SOFTENING TEXTURE

Shiny textures are very "busy" and stimulating, and may even be disturbing if too many are used in one room. This often happens in bathrooms and kitchens. You can create a more calming look by balancing shiny textures with soft and delicate light-filtering textures.

The rough and rustic textures can be very harsh. You need to soften them by using some delicate, light-filtering surfaces alongside them, and bringing in emphasis with some sharp metallic effects.

Soft, light-absorbing textures can sometimes create a claustrophobic feeling, especially if they are on a dark-colored surface. You can avoid this effect by contrasting them with silky, shiny, and light-diffusing textures.

COLOR THERAPY

Color, like sunlight, is a strong mood-enhancer. Wearing favorite colors, or surrounding yourself with them, is a quick and easy way to lift your spirits.

Hospitals and spas use color therapeutically— light, cool colors, for example, have a calming effect. This soothing environment is enlivened with an arrangement incorporating red flowers.

FROM FENG SHUI through to modern color therapy, color has long been associated with healing. The use of color to treat both physical and emotional ills probably dates back to the very earliest of times, and many ancient cultures believed that color had curative qualities. The ancient Egyptians, for instance, used yellow beryl stone to cure jaundice and had temple-based healing centers. The ancient Indians and Chinese also practiced various color-based treatments.

Today color therapy, as a natural healing remedy, is becoming increasingly popular, particularly in New Age circles. The basic idea behind color therapy is the belief that colors, as vibrating wavelengths, react with the body and enter it, acting on the body's cells, and emotions, causing different effects depending on the frequency of vibration. Practitioners believe we can absorb energy from color through our eyes, skin, and breath, or through meditation and visualization.

Color therapists argue that different colors have different therapeutic effects, depending on their wavelength or density, and can be used to treat some illnesses or improve physical or emotional well-being. Yellow, for instance, is said to be helpful for arthritis; green is said to play a part in destroying cancerous cells.

There is no hard and fast evidence to prove this and many doctors either oppose the practice or are sceptical. However, conventional medicine is recognizing the psychological effects of color, and research confirms that color affects mood. For instance, research in the U.S. during the 1970s showed that exposure to red light raised blood pressure and heart rate, while exposure to blue light lowered them. As a result, greater attention is being paid to colors

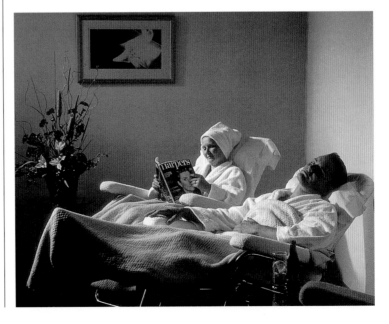

used in hospitals, schools, and prisons. Light-based therapies suggest that ultraviolet light can be used to treat depression, but further scientific research is needed into the therapeutic effects of colored lights.

Many color therapists, calling on ancient Vedic traditions, believe that colors operate vibrations of high frequency that can be seen by some people as an aura of glowing colors around a person, or any living thing. Traditionally, the color of the aura reflects the physical or emotional state of the person it surrounds and will change color, depending on changes in the person.

According to different cultures, particularly those of India, the body contains a number of energy points, known as chakras, each of which is associated with a color. When a person is ill or distressed, the aura becomes imbalanced, and therapy aims to treat the disorder with the appropriate color.

Every day of our lives we are surrounded by color. It is said that if we use it therapeutically it can help us remain healthy throughout our lives.

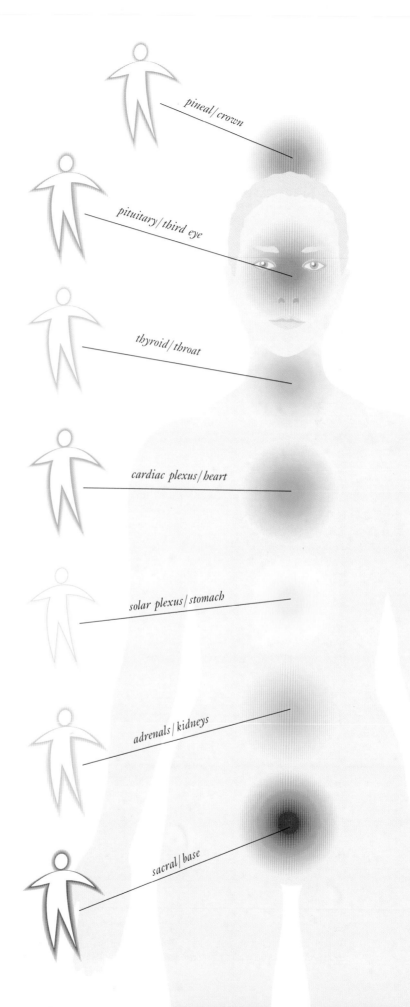

pineal/crown

pituitary/third eye

thyroid/throat

cardiac plexus/heart

solar plexus/stomach

adrenals/kidneys

sacral/base

THE CHARACTERISTICS OF COLOR

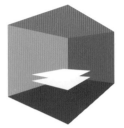

EACH COLOR IN THE SPECTRUM has certain characteristics, and the clever designer or decorator uses them to full advantage. But most colors also have historic, symbolic, and even magical associations, which can vary widely according to culture. Black cats, for instance, are considered lucky in most European countries, whereas in the United States, the reverse is true. Red is the color of fertility in some Asian countries and is used for bridal gowns in India, but green represents fertility to Europeans, as it did to the ancient Egyptians.

BLUE is the color of harmony, peace, and devotion but it can also be an exotic color associated with royalty and wealth. It is usually a cool color, and the paler values in particular will create a sense of space as they bring to mind wide vistas and far horizons.

Blue is fairly low in reflective value, so it will diffuse and soften bright sunlight and calm down a very bright, sunny room. However, blue can be very cold and in the stronger, pure forms can be demanding. Use it with care in small spaces; you may need to warm it up with yellow, red, or orange, especially in cold or north-facing rooms.

The grayed values of blue can be rather dull, so they need contrasting with a warm color and a neutral such as white or cream. The blue/greens can be highly stimulating and exotic; they are associated with rare minerals such as turquoise, jade, and lapis lazuli, as well as peacocks' tails and dragonflies.

Individual colors can improve our health. Blue, a cool, peaceful, and harmonious color, may help reduce stress and relieve tension.

lapis lazuli

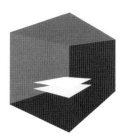

VIOLET and PURPLE also have associations with royalty (imperial purple), but symbolically they represent sensitivity, good taste, and a liking for the arts, music, and philosophy. Purple is also a dignified color, associated with age, and it was a favorite color of mourning in the nineteenth century.

Stronger versions of purple can be vibrant and demanding, so be sure to use them with care. Team them with crisp neutrals, or create a contrast with either cool or warm pastels. Purple is cold when it is on the cool side of the color spectrum, so treat it as you would blue; when purple goes toward red,

it becomes a much warmer color. The paler values—mauves and lilacs—create an impression of space in a room.

Wooden paneling, natural objects, and warm violets and purples make this bathroom a comfortable and relaxing environment, ideal for relieving the strains of a busy day.

A rich red color scheme creates a welcoming and nurturing atmosphere.

The strong appeal of a bowl of strawberries is evidence of the ability of the color red to stimulate appetite.

RED is the warmest advancing color of all and is associated with vitality, energy, and aggressiveness. It is also the color of danger, which is why red is used for fire engines and stop lights. Red can make people feel physically warm, so it is a good color to use in cold rooms.

The stronger values of red can be highly stimulating and overpowering, so use this color with discretion. Red can make a room appear small, intimate, and cozy, but can also be enclosing—even claustrophobic. Red is also an appetite-inducing color, which is why many restaurants are decorated in various versions of red. Consider carefully whether you would want to use red in a dining room.

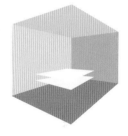

Valentine hearts use pink which is symbolically associated with love, the heart beating with passion.

A combination of cool, sophisticated mauve and pastel pink gives a romantic feel to a bedroom.

When red is mixed with white, it becomes softer and less intense. Traditionally, pink has been associated with love and romance, although this association is not as strong as it once was. As more blue is introduced to the pink, making it mauve or lilac pink, the color becomes more mysterious and sophisticated, useful for creating a cool, spacious ambience.

The deeper, grayed values of red—plum rose and rich burgundy—add richness, elegance, and warmth, without being too overpowering. Like all warm colors, these benefit from the introduction of a little contrast by way of cool color, or definite neutrals such as pure white, black, and clear gray.

The powerful orange of the flower is invigorating and exciting, while the room with the muted orange walls has an earthy, exotic ambience.

Buddhist monks can be recognized from a distance by their bright orange robes. To Buddhists, orange symbolizes humility.

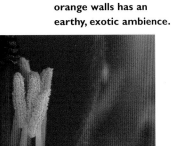

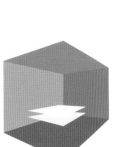

ORANGE brings together the physical energy of red and the intellect of yellow. In its pure form, it is as demanding, intense, and advancing as red. Associated with strength and endurance, orange in Greek mythology was the color attributed to Zeus, the supreme ruler of the gods.

In the East, Buddhist monks wear saffron (bright yellow/orange) robes to symbolize their humility; in Japan, orange is the color of love and happiness.

Orange can be used in the decoration of your home in much the same way as red. It will create a highly stimulating scheme if stronger values are used, and when it is contrasted with black, white, or its complement, blue. Use these strong combinations for children's rooms, to create a welcoming entrance hall, or to warm up a bathroom where you don't want people to linger. Feng shui practitioners, however, would advise against such color combinations.

Pale orange, apricot, and peach are subtle, delicate colors that give a warm and welcoming effect, and can be used in a similar way to pink. Deeper-toned oranges—terracotta, tan, chestnut—are versatile decorating colors. Working like a neutral, they can be used with both warm and cool colors. Used as the main colors with white or cream, they will create a relaxed and warm atmosphere.

You can't help but
be cheered by
springtime yellow
flowers or a bright
yellow room.

YELLOW is a joyful and uplifting color, evocative of summer. The symbolic color of the life-giving sun, yellow is in tune with nature. The clear yellow of spring flowers revives our spirits after the winter months, while deep yellow/golds are associated with the harvest and fruitfulness. Yellow is also associated with creative energy and with intellect and power, and symbolizes wealth. If yellow has a downside, it is the association with illness, such as jaundice, and with the yellow flag of quarantine.

Almost any value of yellow will bring warmth and light into the darkest and coldest room. But bright yellow can be highly stimulating, so use it with care in small spaces. Yellow can create a focal point with a neutral, or cold, contrasting background to set it off. The paler yellows have a high reflective value and will make a small, dark room look much larger, as well as lighter, especially if teamed with subtle blue.

The deeper yellows—mustard, gold, and golden/bronze—are rich, warm, and inviting with a subdued glow. They will help to create an elegant, sophisticated, welcoming atmosphere, and can be contrasted with a clear, neutral or a sharp, cold color. When yellow becomes yellow/green, it can become acid. Some of the deeper, grayed yellow/greens, particularly olive, may appear rich and exciting in daylight, but under artificial light they become dull and gray. These colors therefore should always be exceptionally well lit.

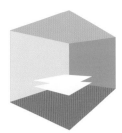

GREEN is the color of nature—and hope! It is associated with green shoots appearing in the spring and the resurgence of nature after winter or drought. In many cultures, green is also the color of fertility. Today, the "green" image also sums up the current refusal to accept pollution and the spoiling of our environment—truly a healthy "green" home.

Coming halfway between the warm and cool colors of the spectrum, green is the color of harmony. It is easy on the eye and creates an atmosphere of relaxation. However, when green is contrasted with its complement red, the result is highly stimulating.

Green recedes, so pale values of green can be used to suggest an impression of space. This color will also bring a verdant, fresh vibrant feel into a sunless basement, apartment, or townhouse in the "concrete jungle" of the city, especially if mid- and deep-toned greens are combined with pale yellow. You can also use green if you wish to bring a feel of nature into the home.

Most greens are cool, but they can be warmed up with a few contrasting accessories and crisp neutrals. Some gray/greens and yellow/greens appear to change color at night, so they need very careful lighting.

In feng shui, green is the color of balance, harmony, and peace. On the color wheel too, it sits midway between cool and warm. Green heralds the arrival of spring and hope; it can have a stabilizing effect.

Vibrant green walls and a mass of plants bring an immediate feeling of nature into this kitchen. Used in the home, green, and its varying shades, can create a fresh, relaxing atmosphere.

BLACK, WHITE, and GRAY

are really the noncolors, but they too, have their own symbolism. Black implies the extinction of all light and color; however, without light there is no life, so pure black is rarely found in nature. It is associated with darkness, witchcraft, and evil, and is almost universally the color of death, grief, mourning, and penitence. Yet, in Western fashion, black is often seen as the height of sophistication and glamour, and black and white is a popular decorating scheme.

Gray is often associated with age and wisdom, as in "gray matter" or *eminence gris*, but it also suggests shadows—pale grays can have an ethereal quality—and sometimes even dullness. Both black and gray are often linked as colors to uniformity, bureaucracy, and institutions.

White is the color of winter and of the moon goddess. It symbolizes innocence, faith, and purity and is associated with chastity and joy, which is why it is the bridal and baptismal color in so many different cultures. White can also be seen as the color of submission and surrender, hence the white flag waved as a sign of truce.

In terms of both design and decoration, apart from being a successful neutral, white is seen as the color of health and hygiene. White is used to suggest and maintain cleanliness in kitchens, bathrooms, food stores, hospitals, and dental and doctors' offices, and it is used for the same reasons in food product packaging.

In fashion, black and white retain an almost timeless sophistication. In feng shui, black is powerful and represents money.

Black and white produce a very chic office space and bedroom in a converted garage. By contrast, muted gray paintwork and neutral walls are more peaceful and appropriate for a dining area.

White can be either stark or restful. Often associated with hygiene, it gives a dramatic and exceptionally clean feel to this very streamlined kitchen.

mauve

blue

Colors that are adjacent in the color wheel are harmonious with each other and can be used together for an attractive decorative scheme.

A monochromatic color scheme can work particularly well in bathrooms, giving a fresh, clean feel, particularly when delicate tones are chosen.

WHEN YOU ARE PLANNING a color scheme, you need to think about many things: the size and shape of the room you are going to decorate, its orientation—that is, which way it faces—and how much natural daylight it receives. Orientation in particular will have an effect on whether you choose warm or cool colors, and whether your colors should be pale, bright, rich, or subtle. You also need to consider the purpose and function of the room, what you are going to use it for, as well as the basic style you are aiming to achieve. You may also need to take into account the architectural style, if any.

A modern kitchen, for example, may well be inviting, attractive, stimulating, and hygienic in pure white, black, and gray with touches of shiny steel and chrome, and strong primary red or orange accents, but such a combination would look out of place in a country cottage kitchen or traditional living room.

TONAL CONTRAST You also need to consider the values and intensity of the colors you choose. If you put too many similar tones together, the effect will lack contrast, so you should aim to combine different tonal values. This is particularly important if you are working with a mono-chromatic (one-color) scheme, or one based on neutrals (yes, neutrals do have different tonal values), or if you are going to decorate your room with mainly plain surfaces, keeping pattern to a minimum.

A warm but
contemporary feel
is achieved in this
living room by
combining mellow
reds and oranges
with a splash
of purple.

The secret of all successful interior design relies on combining the practical with the aesthetic. Therefore, it is often wise to choose the middle and darker tones for those surfaces that will receive the most wear during their lifetime such as the floor and upholstery, and to use the paler colors for the ceiling, walls, woodwork, and areas that are easier to wash or clean. Stronger and pure hues can be introduced into the scheme in the shape of accents and accessories, or can be made use of as an integral part of the design on a patterned item.

BRINGING IN HARMONY

One of the most harmonious color schemes is made by working with different values of one color, to create a monochromatic scheme. Such a scheme will also be calming and relaxing, and, if you use blues or greens, will suggest space and elegance. Again, you should aim for a practical as well as an attractive scheme, relating the strength of the color to the surface on which it is to be used—and the wear and tear it will receive depending upon its location in the home.

Colors that are adjacent on the color wheel naturally harmonize with each other. For example, you could create an attractive scheme based on pale primrose, deep gold, lime, and holly greens, perhaps accented with turquoise (blue/green). You can make both monochromatic and adjacent schemes harmonious if you base them on close color families.

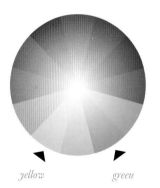

yellow　　　　*green*

**Yellow and green
combine to give an
elegant, harmonious
charm in an
imposing hall.**

orange ▶  ◀ *blue*

BRINGING IN CONTRAST

Contrasting or complementary color schemes are the most stimulating and should be used for areas where you do not want to sit and relax. You can create contrasting schemes by using two dynamic opposites: yellow/violet, red/green, or blue/orange; but again think about achieving tonal contrast and the use of a neutral as a link. Pale primrose combined with rich plum purple and cream as the neutral; deep Indian red contrasted with pale apple green and sparked with white; lapis-lazuli blue with terracotta and pale silver gray—all are complementary schemes. A simpler way of creating a contrasting scheme is to combine a warm with a cool color, which need not necessarily be complete opposites, blue with yellow, for example.

Contrasting color schemes enliven and stimulate a living space, but can also provide a harmonious feel. You can create contrasts by taking two dynamic opposites or by blending cool and warm colors. More complex schemes involve using three contrasting colors.

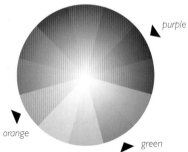

purple ▶
◀ *orange*
▶ *green*

Tricks of the trade

Whichever type of scheme you choose —whether it is based on mainly warm or mainly cool colors, a monochromatic tone, or a subtle blend of neutrals— remember one of the tricks used by the professionals: add a few sharp contrasts with vases, towels, kitchenware, and other accessories to strengthen the effect you have created.

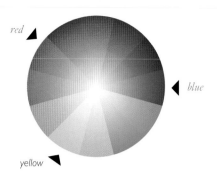

red ◀

blue ◀

yellow ◀

A triad of the primary colors—red, yellow, and blue—gives a colorful scheme that need not be overpowering if carefully chosen.

THREE-COLOR SCHEMES

It is possible to make contrasting schemes that are more complex. A triadic scheme, for example, is based on the use of three colors that are equidistant on the color wheel. You may choose to use the primaries of red, yellow, and blue to create a very stimulating scheme, which is sometimes appropriate for children's rooms. Or you could use three secondaries such as orange, green, and violet; or even three of the tertiary colors such as blue/green, red/violet, and yellow/orange. Again, it is not necessary to use the pure hues, as more subtle values of the colors will still create a contrast.

A split complementary scheme is one that combines either a primary or a secondary color with the two colors that are positioned on each side of its complement, so red combined with blue/green and yellow/green, orange mated with blue/violet and blue/green, yellow with red/violet and blue/violet, and so on are all split complementary schemes, even if different tints, tones, and shades of the colors are mixed and are used.

MOOD MAKING

STYLE AND COLOR SCHEMES APART, when you choose and use color, you are also aiming to create a particular mood or ambience. Color in its own right creates atmosphere; pattern and texture can add an extra visual dimension and help to set the style of the room.

The moods you create with color reflect the characteristics of the individual colors. Using color you can create rooms that feel warm or cold, spacious or intimate, exciting or restful. The choice is yours, depending on your needs and aims.

CREATING A FEELING OF SPACE

The cool colors of the spectrum work well in warm, sunny south- and west-facing rooms, giving an impression of elegance, and, in their paler values, a spacious feel. Strong, cold colors can also be uncomfortable and can be used to prevent people from lingering in a room, especially if the cool tones are combined with a strong contrasting warm color.

If you prefer a calm, elegant look, opt for the cooler greens, blue/greens, blue, indigo, purple — the receding or short-wavelength colors, which seem to go away from you. These are also space makers and will help to increase the size of an area visually, especially if you use paler values such as powder blue, mint green, silver/sage, lilac, pale green/grays.

For a spacious look, too, choose a scheme based on a blue, blue/green, green, lilac, or cool gray; to introduce a little warmth, work with yellow, gold, and touches of brass: pink, rose, and subtle red; pale peach, terracotta, and copper—always within the same color segment.

Cool, spacious schemes can sometimes lack interest. To counter this, introduce a neutral color, and at least one colorful, contrasting accessory or accent. Think about adding a touch of Indian red, ocher, or sizzling pink to pastel blues or subtle green, rich tones to contrast with creamy neutrals. A patterned surface, too, perhaps in the form of wall coverings, flooring, curtains, or upholstery fabrics, can add contrast to the main colors.

A room decorated in a neutral/off-white scheme will have an open, airy feeling and a sense of light—even if the room is dark. Any touch of color will be highlighted. Light-toned wood is a natural complement to cream and off-white, harmonizing without drawing focus.

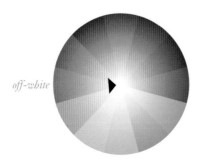

off-white

light-toned peach

CREATING A FEELING OF WARMTH

All the warm colors—in their various tints, tones, and shades—will suggest a feeling of well-being. They work particularly well in cold, dark, and north- or west-facing rooms. The warm colors can be used to create a cozy, intimate ambience, and to make a vast area, such as the entrance hall in a large older property, seem smaller and more welcoming to visitors and to those who live there.

Use the advancing or dominant hues to achieve this intimate and warm effect. These include the warm, long-wavelength colors such as red/violet, red, red/orange, orange, yellow/orange yellow, and some yellow/greens. You can also use their various tints, tones, and shades, such as pink, rose, wine red, peace, gold, apricot, yellow, and terracotta, to create the same result.

For that added touch, you can drop strong, cool accents into a mainly warm scheme. Jade, peacock, and sky blue, for instance, can be used successfully with peach or terracotta.

Warm tones like salmon and peach can make even this large space seem cozy and comfortable.

Getting the right match

Color matching should never be a hit-or-miss affair. When you are searching for the various components of your color scheme, the only way to ensure an accurate color match is to take samples of existing items with you. If you are looking for color to match existing floor, walls, curtains, or furniture, take a sample of the carpet or other fabric with you, bearing in mind that it may have faded through time. You can also take pieces of colored paper, woods, embroidery thread, or ribbon.

Don't match to photographs or leaflets because color printing is rarely accurate. Instead, ask suppliers or retailers for fabric, flooring, or wallpaper samples, as large as possible, and take them home so you can look at them against the original items in both day and night lighting.

With paint or stain for walls, woodwork, floor, and ceiling, buy a small amount, if little tester cans are unavailable, and paint it onto a spare piece of wood. Try to do as large a sample as possible to get a realistic picture.

105

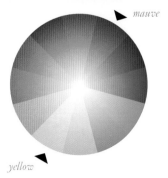

mauve

yellow

CREATING EXCITEMENT
The way you put colors together is called creating color harmonies, although sometimes you may be wanting to create excitement rather than harmony. For instance, if you want to achieve a stimulating effect, perhaps in a children's playroom or in a room where you want people to move on, such as the bathroom, use contrasting or complementary colors.

Try combining a warm with a cool color, such as red with green, blue with orange, purple with yellow. These are all direct opposites on the color wheel, and can be very strong and dominant.

You can create a softer but still stimulating scheme by using pale and subtle values of the complementary colors or by teaming yellow and blue or gray and pink.

You can create an exciting color scheme for a child's bedroom by combining contrasting colors, such as purple and yellow. If the effect is too dramatic, soften it with subtler values of the same colors.

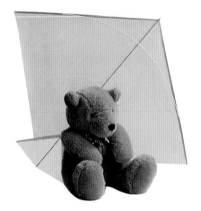

It is a good idea to add plenty of textural contrast to exciting, stimulating schemes. To do this, combine shiny light-reflecting surfaces with rough, rustic, and matt light-absorbing ones. Also try to introduce some delicate, light-diffusing effects such as sheer fabrics, lace panels, slatted blinds, cane, and wickerwork.

CREATING CALM AND RELAXATION
If the effect you want to achieve is a calm, relaxed ambience, work with colors from the same family, colors which are found next to each other in the spectrum or beside each other on the color wheel.

To create a sense of calm, try working with yellow/green, green/blue, and green. Alternatively, you could work up a scheme with rose, lilac, lavender, and blue, or introduce more warmth by using yellow with yellow/orange, tans, and terracotta.

Calm schemes such as these may include mainly warm or mainly cool colors; this will depend on which segment of the color wheel you choose. They may even be a combination of both, in which case the scheme would become more stimulating.

For an even more relaxing theme, work up a monochromatic color scheme. This type of harmony is based on different values of one basic hue, so you need to work within only one segment of the color wheel. However, to ensure the effect is not too bland, make sure there is plenty of tonal contrast.

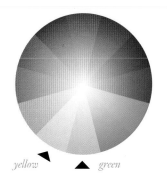

Opposing colors stimulate and excite; adjacent colors are calmer and more relaxing.

yellow ▲   ▲ *green*

USING
NEUTRALS
You can also use neutrals and natural textures to create a relaxing area, but make sure they come from the same color family. The only true neutrals are black, white, and gray (made by mixing white together in different proportions to create different values), but these three non-colors used together can be highly stimulating, especially if they are combined with bold patterns and lots of different textures.

These days there are other "accepted" neutrals, even though some may have a different color bias. They include cream, beige, off-white, taupe, mushroom, brown and the colors of natural, untreated materials, such as wood, sisal, hemp, seagrass, jute, slate, clay, undyed canvas, linen, cotton, and gauze.

There are also different "natural whites," usually created by taking a large amount of white, very pale gray or cream, and adding a small amount of color. The result is usually a rather wishy-washy version of the original color, which looks almost like white. The color will, in reality, be bluish, greenish, pinkish, or even yellow-toned, and needs very careful color-matching, because the original color becomes more obvious when seen in relation to other colors in the scheme.

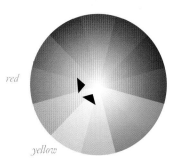

red

▲
 ▲

yellow

Depending on its shade, blue can produce a cool, stylish atmosphere, although darker values can be vibrant. More neutral colors, such as beige, cream, or mushroom used with natural materials, help to create a calm, relaxed room.

ADDING
A THIRD
DIMENSION

You can create bold patterns by grouping floor tiles in zigzags and introducing furniture in contrasting shapes. But confine them to less-used areas.

Too much pattern in a kitchen can be tiring. Limit it to checkered floor tiles, with objects and furniture creating interest.

A SUCCESSFUL ROOM scheme includes not only color but also an effective use of pattern combined with textural and tonal contrasts. Like color, patterns can help to create calm feelings, or they can excite you, or entice you, drawing you into a room. Patterns can also appear to change the proportions of a space, and suggest a modern or period flavor.

Bold patterns work like warm colors; they tend to advance, so appear to be coming toward you. They give a room a stimulating and exciting feel. They should be used with care, and they work best in large, cold spaces or on large surfaces. Small patterns are like cool, pale colors; they seem to recede and go away from you. They will create an impression of space, but very small miniprint patterns tend to fade into insignificance if used over a large area. To keep this from happening, you may prefer to opt for an interesting texture rather than a design.

The use of pattern can also help to set a specific style, either a period flavor or more modern ambience. The right choice of pattern and color can enhance and echo the original architectural style. It can emphasize important features or bring character and presence into what might otherwise be a rather bland space.

But what exactly is pattern? It can be a linear design, printed or hand-applied on fabrics, wall-coverings, floorings, or ceramic tiles, or a design woven into fabrics, stenciled onto walls, furniture, or woodwork, or added to ceilings with decorative plasterwork. Even furniture can suggest pattern.

Patterns can also be made by grouping together several objects or similar items. Individual floor or wall tiles, for example, may be plain individually but can be grouped together to create a pattern. Grouped tiles, for instance, can create bold and geometric patterns, especially if different or contrasting colors are used, or if some tiles are cut into triangles or light and dark tiles are laid in a distinctive checkerboard pattern.

An arrangement of various objects, pictures grouped on a wall, a miscellany of pillows thrown onto a sofa or bed can also create patterns, provided they are made of contrasting colors and forms. Such patterning is flexible because you can change or alter it as you wish. It can also be calmer and more harmonious than the use of bold design.

Feng shui uses patterns to activate different energies. Checks and squares boost earth energy; rectangles activate wood energy.

Pattern through time

Incorporating pattern into a decorating scheme always needs careful consideration, and the use of pattern has changed considerably over the centuries. During the 18th century, pattern was usually restricted to fabrics and carpets, or created by the use of decorative plasterwork and grouping of patterned china, but in the early 19th century pattern was provided by wallpaper panels as well as on fabrics. By the mid-1800s rooms were a riot of pattern. In a kind of backlash, the Arts and Crafts movement called for plainer surfaces, with the pattern interest added in fabrics, rugs, and furniture. During the early 1920s, plain walls and floors were popular, but in the mid-1920s and 1930s geometric and decorative Art Deco designs were woven into rugs and printed on fabrics. The Bauhaus influence and the minimalist look of the 1930s, succeeded by the hi-tech style of the 1950s, relied more on texture and color, although bold geometric patterns were used for wallpapers and fabrics. Most recently, a well-balanced scheme has usually consisted of two, or at the most three, patterned surfaces, although the vogue for co-ordinated and companion lines has made it possible to use the same pattern—or the positive and negative of the same design — on several items from wall coverings to flooring.

Like color, pattern falls into two main types: those that advance and stimulate, and those that recede and create a calming influence. Neutral patterns can be used to make visual links between patterned surfaces, or on their own. These include the checks, stripes, plaids, miniprints, and quiet geometrics, which are often timeless.

When choosing a pattern, think about its design and scale, and the surface on which you will use it. Heavily patterned walls and bold carpet designs can be dominant. Patterned drapes, which hang in folds, can be more flexible and fluid, and create interesting designs when the drapes are drawn. Patterned drapes against plain walls can be effective, as can a bold plain color against patterned walls. If you prefer your windows to blend in with the rest of the decor, choose curtains that coordinate with the wall coverings.

TAKING CARE There are certain areas in a home where it is not wise to use too strong a pattern —on kitchen work surfaces for example, where they can cause eyestrain. Wall tiles in bathrooms and kitchens need careful selection— too bold a pattern will become irritating, but tiles are difficult to remove if you change your mind.

Walls are another surface where too bold a design can become difficult to live with. Also, as walls are often not completely square, the pattern can appear to be slipping off the wall. Always look at wall coverings unwrapped, and with at least two widths side by side to assess the overall effect. Floor tiles should be seen in a mirrored box, which suggests a whole floor. A very bold design on a carpet, particularly in the hall, stairs, landing, and main rooms of a home, can seem to rise up at you every time you open the door!

The use of local building materials and traditional architectural styles dictates the color schemes and appearance of these French houses.

THE TRADITION of painting the inside of our dwelling places goes back to prehistoric times, when early peoples painted the walls of their caves. And archeologists have proved that early forms of architecture, such as Aztec pyramids, were either faced with metal and ceramics or covered in painted frescoes. This made them stand out as "important" buildings, and frequently the colors chosen were highly symbolic.

Temples, palaces, and other buildings in ancient Egypt and Greece were often brightly painted—the Parthenon (432 BC) was painted in bright red, blue, and pink, with gilding applied to the friezes above the white lime-washed columns that may have symbolized virginity.

At the height of the Art Deco period in Britain, Europe, and the U.S.—which took much of its inspiration from Egypt after the discovery of Tutankhamen's tomb in 1922—this look was copied. Buildings by Gaudi in Spain, for example, were often clad in colorful ceramics, and the famous Hoover factory in Middlesex, England, which was built in

the 1930s, is a combination of white and bright reds, blues, greens, and gold—a "temple," in essence, to the vacuum cleaner.

But color is not only used for public buildings—paint and various color washes have been used for centuries to decorate and protect the walls and beams of our houses.

Historically, villages, towns, and cities were built from local materials and, until the end of the 18th century, were painted with pigments made from local deposits of earth. The colors depended on geographical location: rich ocher yellow and terracotta colors are typical of certain regions in France, and "Suffolk Pink" is a strong color relating to the clay present in Britain's Suffolk soil.

When planning colors for the exterior of your home, particularly the façade, try to choose a scheme that will be in harmony with the environment. In a rural environment, you could collect and analyze local soil samples and collect examples of the predominant building materials. Check these against an exterior paint chart—you will find several manufacturers have produced lines that were inspired by various regional or historical colors.

In the country, local stone, flint, or slate might be used for the main construction. When local brick kilns were established, the bricks would have been used locally and would therefore be in keeping with the environment. It was only when bricks started to be transported— by canal and then by rail—that

This French country house blends perfectly with its surroundings; insensitive modernization would completely ruin its appearance.

Contrasting primary
colors harmonize
well in a hot, sunny
climate but would be
unsuitable for colder,
northern regions.

brick buildings became out of tune with their surroundings. Some farm buildings were painted with local pigments for the purpose of camouflaging them, so they would fade into the surrounding background or earth.

Today it is considered poor design to cover a building with something not in keeping with the houses in the surrounding area. In a simple brick-built row of houses for example, a stone façade stands out like a sore thumb, as does any other example of overimproving, which includes many replacement windows (and bull's-eye panes); overornate front doors, fences, and gates; false beams; and phony plastic pillars, columns, and porticoes. On the other hand, any original architectural detail should be preserved and enhanced whenever possible.

There is no reason why simple houses should not be painted in attractive colors. In Italy, Greece, the South of France, Spain, Mexico, and Portugal, exteriors are often colorfully painted or sided with ceramics. Of course, these are seen under strong, bright sunlight most of the time, and against a pure blue sky. In northern cities, strong, clear colors can sometimes appear too brash.

Care should be taken not to create a scheme that will clash with the surrounding houses. The combination of colors for the façade, woodwork, rainwater pipes and gutters, eaves, front gate, and fence or railings needs to be worked out with as much care as a color scheme for an individual room in the home would be. It is possible to use color outside to improve the proportions of a building visually. For example, a tall, narrow house can be made to look wider, and a small, squat building can be made to appear taller than it really is.

AND SOUND

Once you have planned your home to function efficiently, banished all clutter, chosen suitable color schemes, and sorted out the lighting, it is time to spoil yourself. A healthy home should be somewhere to relax, enjoy your surroundings, and pamper yourself. So if you have always wanted to sleep in silk sheets, surround your bathtub with scented candles, or play and sing along with your preferred type of music—go for it.

Pleasing sounds encourage relaxation—the natural sounds of bird song and flowing water, the tinkling of strategically placed wind chimes, even recorded sounds of waves, are soothing and smooth away stress that has accumulated during the day. Playing a musical instrument can be very therapeutic, and if you don't play an instrument, make time to listen to your favorite music and relax. Silence, too, is essential for physical and emotional health—a house full of jarring, continuous noise is not conducive to relaxation.

Clean, pure air flowing through the home encourages health. Make sure the air in your home is not polluted; check humidity, temperature levels, and ventilation. A moving flow of air can refresh in summer, but be too chilling in winter. You may want to consider air conditioning, or ionizers and humidifiers to purify the air if anyone in the family has breathing problems.

You can enhance air quality and atmosphere in your home with scented candles, oils, sweet-smelling flowers and herbs, and potpourri, but always use natural products. Consider drying your own herbs; their scent adds pleasure to the home, and many have specific health-giving qualities.

Think about how you want your home to feel. Touch is an important sensation; the textures you use in your home can make it more sensuous—velvet or silk drapes, satin sheets, shaggy pile rugs, chenille upholstery, fur fabric pillows are all eminently strokeable. Juxtapose them with metallic or light-filtering textiles to provide tactile and visual contrast. The patina of beautifully polished furniture is both pleasing to the eye and wonderful to touch.

Use natural materials in your home—pure cotton sheets, lace and voile drapes, soft covers on bedside tables, cotton curtains, and natural woods.

Water, too, creates a soothing or sensuous mood. Use it in the yard or on a patio, or create water features inside. Whirlpool, massage baths, and showers ease muscular pains and sooth away stress and tension. A long, hot soak in a bathtub, filled with scented water and lit by candlelight, with your favorite drink close at hand, can be the height of pleasure. You might even like to install a sauna for deep cleanliness.

REDUCING NOISE

No house can ever be totally silent; without some sounds it would lack life and be almost sepulchral. But quietness and peace are essential for relaxation and health. A noisy house is not a relaxing one, and it may be necessary to seek adequate sound insulation for your home.

Noise—or unwanted sound—bombards us constantly and can have a very negative effect on our health, causing irritation, stress, and even physical ailments. Some noise penetrates the home from outside, perhaps from nearby roads, schools, garages, airports, or railroads. If you live in an apartment or row of houses, you may also experience noise from neighbors—remember that your noise can be equally distracting to them.

Families can create their own noise pollution, shouting, arguing, and playing music without regard to others. Today, most modern homes are also filled with noise-generating technology—answering machines and early morning alarms bleep at us; dishwashers and washing machines can be extremely intrusive, particularly when they reach their "spin" cycle; telephones and televisions can be intolerable; and vacuum cleaners cause an unpleasant drone.

For the sake of a healthy home, you will need some form of noise control to prevent unwanted sounds from traveling up and down through floors, ceilings, and walls. Whole-house planning is a sensible start to cutting down on noise problems, allocating rooms or using them according to their noise impact. For instance, avoid putting heavy-footed, music-playing teenagers above their grandmother's bedroom, the main bedroom, or next to a nursery. If space allows, you may even be able to create a separate music room, perhaps in the garage, although realistically most of us live in fairly small properties; we rarely have enough room to provide special facilities and have to work with what we have.

NOISE INSULATION

Noise travels through floorboards and along floor joists so a thick layer of insulation between joists, floor and ceiling will help to deaden sound. Carpet or carpet tiles also absorb noise, especially if they are laid over a dense underlay. If carpet is not a practical choice, because of hygiene or if family members suffer from allergies, choose a quiet-inducing-surface underfoot. Cork, rubber, or linoleum—even cushioned vinyl—will be "bouncier" and less noisy than wood, ceramic tiles, slate, and other hard floorings, but for good feng shui, you should avoid artificial materials. Floorings such as wood or slate are natural materials and can be softened with rugs to muffle sound more; make sure they have nonslip backings or use washable cotton rugs.

Noise also passes through house walls; solid walls in particular transmit sound efficiently. To reduce the amount of sound, you can effectively insulate the wall by creating a second layer and leaving a space between that and the wall. You can line walls with wood, perhaps using tongue-and-groove in a country-style kitchen or bathroom, or laminated panels, particularly in a modern bathroom. You can also use special insulated compressed fiberboard to cover walls, and then decorate the fiberboard, using either paint or wallpaper. As boards are mounted on the wall, you can leave as much space between the two layers as is practical. You can also muffle sound by placing insulating board behind cupboards or closets. Of course, closets full of clothes can make a useful natural sound barrier.

Consider using equipment at a time when it would be less offensive to the ear.

Perceived decibels	Typical sounds
140–130	**Threshold of pain** Jet engine at 100 feet; pneumatic riveter; hydraulic press at 3 feet
120	**Threshold of injury** Sandblasting; loud thunder
110	Discotheque speakers at 4 feet; pneumatic drill
100	Food blender at 2 feet; nearby chainsaw or motorcycle
90	Heavy truck; automatic lathe
80	**Danger level** Heavy city traffic; factory noise; alarm clock at 2 feet; subway
70	Busy shopping street; large department store; building noise; vacuum cleaner, food mixer, washing machine
60	Normal conversation at 3 feet
50	Quiet street; inside average home
40	Quiet office; quiet conversation, residential area at night; refrigerator; bedroom away from traffic
30	Ticking watch; rustle of paper; whispered conversation
20	Quiet country lane
10	Leaves rustling in wind
0	**Threshold of hearing**

Living on a busy road or at a frequently backed-up intersection can be stressful because of noise. Proper insulation and careful decorating can protect your ears and peace of mind.

NOISE CONTROL

Thick curtains at an outside window provide two types of insulation—against cold drafts and noise. They also prevent indoor noise from disturbing those outside!

A window shade can enhance the insulating properties of curtains. Four-poster beds with full curtains have been used for centuries to keep out the cold.

FABRIC SOLUTIONS

Fabric also softens sound. Fabric-covered walls therefore act as sound barriers and are decorative. Fabric is usually put on walls by stretching it over strips of wood, or attaching it to a special track. The fabric is slipped into place between two flanges, and can be pleated in position for an elegant appearance.

Uncovered windows let in sound as well as cold. Heavy, lined curtains provide good insulation against both; they absorb sound and guard against drafts. They also prevent heat and noise from escaping through the window. Floor-to-ceiling and possibly wall-to-wall drapes, combined with blinds close to the glass, will act as an extra insulatory layer.

If you have a severe noise, and possibly weather, problem, you will need to consider double or even triple glazing for windows. For this to be fully effective, you should have a gap of at least 4 inches (ideally 6–8 inches) between the layers of glass. Laminated glass is a good idea in sunrooms and for glazed front and back doors, both for safety, if there are children in the house, and also if burglaries are a possibility.

A ceiling lavishly tented with fabric is exotic and alluring, and will help to deaden sound. A canopy above a bed with side drapes has the same attractions—it is exotic and reduces unwanted noise. Interestingly, the original four-poster bed with drapes was designed for such purposes—to keep out drafts, make bedfellows warm and cozy, and deaden sound from outside, and inside, the drapes. When this type of bed was originally invented, there was rarely a separate bed chamber, and the bed was positioned on an upper gallery of a "hall house"—usually one giant room with a fire in the center, a hole in the roof for smoke, and an upper gallery for a little privacy. Today, feng shui practitioners recommend a canopy and side drapes or four-poster bed for those having difficulty relaxing and switching off from the stresses of the day.

Hard-textured surfaces such as ceramic tiled walls and floors, slate, quarry tiles, marble, wood, laminated, granite and steel counters all reflect sound and increase decibel levels—as a result, kitchens and bathrooms are often the noisiest rooms in the house, apart from teenage bedrooms. You can offset this by adding soft textures—large, fluffy, washable cotton rugs to a bathroom and a square of rush matting or sisal to the kitchen floor, or use cork, rubber, or cushioned vinyl as hygienic and softer alternatives to hard flooring.

You could also consider a "floating floor"; this consists of a floor surface that rests on a resilient pad positioned above the main structural floor. Cork or laminated floorings are often best laid in this way. Adding an enclosed porch to the front entrance or to the back door will also cut down on noise and drafts.

If you have a balcony that you rarely use because of outside noise you could glass it in to reduce external noise, and to make a place for green plants.

CONSIDERING OTHERS
Finally, environmental harmony is also about considering others and their health needs, and taking active steps to reduce any noise pollution that you may produce. As a good neighbor, you should not carry out structural or do-it-yourself work early in the morning or late at night. If you have builders working for you, discuss this with them, and make sure they keep radios at an acceptable level. Warn immediate neighbors of any building work or late-night parties. Work toward harmony with your neighbors by using your household appliances during the day rather than at night, not plumbing them into party walls or insulating the wall behind them, and keeping doors shut to prevent unwanted sounds from escaping.

Practical tips
• Save any spare carpet or carpet tiles and place them, in layers, underneath the television, radio, music system, or keyboard to absorb sound.
• If you are replacing windows, make sure they are adequately insulated from noise as well as cold and drafts.

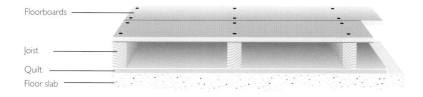

Floorboards

Joist

Quilt

Floor slab

A floating floor, created by placing floorpads between the floorboards and the structural floor, is an effective way of reducing noise.

USING SOUND CREATIVELY

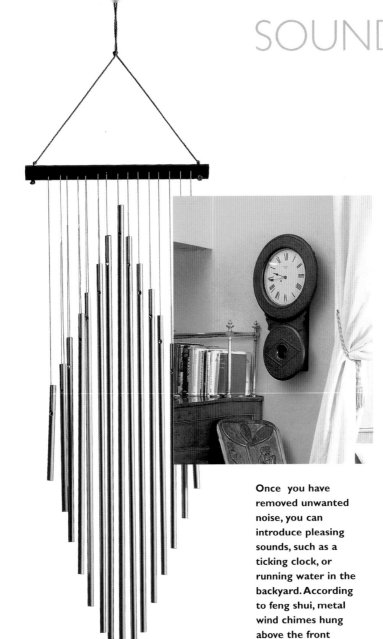

Once you have removed unwanted noise, you can introduce pleasing sounds, such as a ticking clock, or running water in the backyard. According to feng shui, metal wind chimes hung above the front door purify the atmosphere.

INTRODUCING SOUND into the home can stimulate, soothe, relax, reduce stress and tension, and calm frayed nerves. You can use natural or human-made sounds, from the tinkling of water splashing over pebbles to the melodious sound of the harp or cello or the human voice reading a story or crooning a lullaby. Other sounds, too, can be comforting—a clock ticking or chiming, doves cooing, or a cat purring.

There are many recordings and tapes available of natural sounds, which you can choose to suit your mood and the ambience of a room. The sounds of the sea and waves ebbing and flowing across the shale, a babbling brook, or the crisper sound of a splashing fountain can be effective and invigorating in the bathroom or shower, or more relaxing in a sunroom. Birdsong is a far better and more stimulating noise to wake up to than the strident notes of an alarm clock; soothing bird song is a welcoming sound in a dining room, or in the backyard for meals eaten alfresco on the patio. Relaxing sounds are also appropriate in the bedroom and will help to prepare you for a good night's sleep.

CHIMING SOUNDS
Sound vibrates the air, stimulating the flow of chi energy, and for this reason it plays an important part in feng shui. For good feng shui you can use specific sounds to stimulate the energy in areas such as dark corners, under sloping roofs, and in halls and corridors, and to prevent

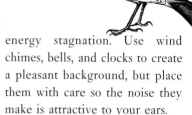

energy stagnation. Use wind chimes, bells, and clocks to create a pleasant background, but place them with care so the noise they make is attractive to your ears.

Wind chimes are made from several different materials—metal, wood, or ceramic. Metal chimes tend to sound clear and slightly mysterious, like a hidden flute player; ceramic chimes are more brittle; and wooden or bamboo chimes can create a softer sound, although some may appear dull and muffled. Decide where in the house and/or yard you want to site your chimes, then choose the most suitable material by checking the direction from the center of the house. For good feng shui, metal chimes are best sited in the garden. If hung near the entrance, where noise pollution may be a problem, they help to alter the vibrations coming into the home.

Bells and gongs can be used to clear any stagnant or heavy areas of energy in the house and to stimulate the chi energy. A gong, hung in the hall near the center of the home, will reverberate throughout the whole house when struck, which is why they have been traditionally used to summon family or guests to meals. Choose one with a deep melodious tone.

Bells can be rung by hand in any area where you want to enhance the flow of chi energy. Nonelectric doorbells can also stimulate and help to keep the chi energy force fresh and clear. Avoid doorbells that play a tune.

The regularity of a ticking and chiming clock will help to create a more ordered chi energy and may help you to lead a more orderly life—the ticking broken by the occasional chime will be more stimulating and will clear chi energy periodically.

OUTDOOR SOUNDS

Plants can also help to absorb sounds; their placing is an integral part of feng shui, so they must be put in appropriate locations. Some plants make an attractive noise: the rustling of leaves on broad-leafed trees, the sound of the wind in a border of grasses or bamboo, even reeds if you have a water feature will all sound pleasingly natural. Such sounds will be more obvious out of doors, unless your windows are wide open, but avoid planting large trees or tall grasses too close to the house. A small sapling soon becomes a large tree, which can cut daylight. Spreading roots may also interfere with drains or the foundations, so check their final height before planting.

And of course if you plant flowers, trees, and shrubs that attract birds and insects, the happy, hazy drone of bees in spring and summer, and the birds' dawn chorus, will percolate into your home. If you are incredibly lucky, a nightingale may even serenade you in the evening, something that you could record to replay in the winter months. If appropriate, you could also install a dovecote, but remember that doves can cause damage to mortar in brick-built chimneys and to the pointing between courses of bricks.

Many of us have fairly stressed lives that can damage our health. Listening to outdoor sounds such as the cooing of doves or the rustling of bamboo provides much-needed calm and an important link with the natural world.

INDOOR SOUNDS If as a family you enjoy making music and playing various musical instruments, there is no greater way of relaxing than to create your own harmonies. A well-tuned grand piano, a string quartet, the melodious sounds of the cello and harp, the silvery tones of a flute will all give immense pleasure and enjoyment to both listeners and participants. And there is no reason why family music-making should be confined to the more classical approach—you can play jazz, rock, or any other type of music that turns you on. But again, consider the neighbors and insulate them from unwanted noise.

SOUND SYSTEMS Most homes today contain music systems for playing music, relaxation tapes, and so on. Constant music can be irritating for others, so make sure your system is flexible, with effec-

Forget your daily cares for an hour and lose yourself in music, but consider other people in the home and do not play it too loudly or, alternatively, use a set of earphones.

Speakers placed to form a triangle

tive volume control. As with any other appliances, do not place a music system too close to a party wall or directly on a hard floor. Stand it on an insulated surface, so that sound is contained in one area.

If you want all-around sound, you will need to site your speakers carefully. If you are buying a very sophisticated system, the supplier will advise on installation, and if your home is designed and decorated in a particular period style, you may prefer to conceal the speakers in the ceiling, in built-in furniture, or behind a baffle. If you are setting up the system in the bedroom, speakers could be built into the headboard, concealed behind it, or positioned on top shelves in the closet.

If you use wall- or floor-mounted speakers, try to screen them in some way; use plants to camouflage floor-mounted speakers; wall-mounted speakers could be an integral part of a storage wall, where they will fade into the background. In a modern, hi-tech,

or minimalist setting, placing the music system and speakers on three-wheel trolleys can provide a flexible, stylish arrangement.

For good listening, place your speakers equidistant from the area where you are most likely to sit, or recline, so you form a triangle with your seating at the apex. The length of the sides of the triangle should be at least two yards, but should be in proportion to the size of the longest wall in the room.

You can have a conveniently positioned music deck as the

"nerve center" of your music system, relaying music to all parts of the house and yard, via concealed cabling and strategically positioned speakers. It can be very pleasant to listen to music in the bathtub or when relaxing in the bedroom; music can be an energizing addition to the kitchen when you are cooking and a pleasing background sound when entertaining in the dining room. The type of music you choose to play at any time will reflect the mood and atmosphere you are hoping to create.

Again, even if your home is a property with a yard, you need to consider noise pollution and the neighbors, and make sure your house is well insulated for outgoing sounds. Keep a firm hand on the volume control button, especially if teenagers are using the system!

You can use timers to preset a radio, music system, and lighting to come on after dark—a good security device.

Nothing sets the mood like music. Your music stereo, whether it is a small portable or an expensive sound system, can create the relaxing atmosphere that you need.

THE SOUND
OF WATER

WATER IS ESSENTIAL for life and health. The sound of moving water in and around the home encourages relaxation, meditation, and well-being. Water has also long been used as a design feature.

Outside the home, water features, with water flowing from a fountain, gushing from a gargoyle's mouth, or trickling over pebbles from level to level, will all make your backyard a more relaxing place. Swimming pools, too, can be a source of great enjoyment, although remember that they can be noise pollutants in their own right. Their hard surfaces create a natural echo chamber and the shrieks of children or of evening swimmers can annoy neighbors. Build changing areas or a filtration house to create a sound barrier; evergreen trees planted near a pool can also serve to muffle sound.

You may choose to introduce water features indoors. These will be particularly effective in a home in the heart of the city, where there may be no access to a garden. A fountain or water sculpture will enhance a sunroom or entrance hall; it could be equally effective in the dining or living room, even the bedroom or study. You may also be able to install a water feature on a balcony or roof terrace, surrounded by moisture-loving plants. The noise of constantly running water can be irritating, so make sure the water can be turned off easily.

As with any decorative feature, think about enhancing a water feature with good lighting; the light catching the drops of water gushing from a fountain will look like an expensive chandelier—you might even get a rainbow as a bonus. A fish tank can also provide a water feature and is calming in its own right.

Water sustains life, and its healing qualities are well known. In your home, the gentle sound of water trickling from one level to another is soothing.

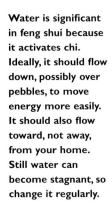

Water is significant in feng shui because it activates chi. Ideally, it should flow down, possibly over pebbles, to move energy more easily. It should also flow toward, not away, from your home. Still water can become stagnant, so change it regularly.

WATER AND
FENG SHUI

Water plays an important role in feng shui. It is a powerful activator of the chi energy force and also has a special significance for health. By adding water features to house and yard, you will bring in fresh energy. The water feature can be any of those discussed above, but even a birdbath or bowl of clean water can improve the atmosphere and energy. The water must always be fresh and unpolluted, so will need to be changed regularly or refilled once a day.

A waterfall, with the water falling downward rather than gushing upward from a fountain, will be more calming, and water flowing over pebbles, or along the bed of a stream, circumnavigating stones, statuary, and other features, will move chi energy more easily. The sounds will be particularly soothing and can help you through

stressful stages in your life. Any fountain or water feature can also help to protect you from fast-moving energy generated by a busy road, or from the cutting chi caused by the sharp corners of another building, but it must be positioned between the heart of the home and the source of bad chi. You should aim to place water features in such a way that they balance the five elements.

A garden pond should be circular, kidney-shaped, or curved in some way. Avoid sharp corners and angles, plant the pond with special plants to increase oxygenation, and introduce frogs, fish, and other aquatic animals to maintain a good ecological balance. Constantly moving water incorporated into the pond via a fountain or some other source will help to keep the water fresh and clean and will prevent stagnation.

For good feng shui, swimming pools also need careful shaping and siting. Again, use circular, curved, or kidney shapes. If a rectangular or square shape is unavoidable, soften the shape with rounded corners. It should be sited in the most favorable direction—east or southeast from the center of the home—but you also need to consider the amount of sun and shade the pool will receive. Try not to position it too close to the house walls or immediately opposite a door leading into your home. If you build an indoor pool, it should be sited in the east or southeast of your home, and it should be well ventilated so damp and condensation will not cause stagnation in the pool area and in the rest of the house. Divide the pool off from the rest of the house, and keep dividers and doors firmly closed.

Outdoors, moving water should flow toward, not away, from your front door, ideally flowing toward it in gentle curves—if water flows away, it can take prosperity from the home.

Design and architecture have incorporated water for centuries. Water features as dramatic as this are most likely to be a feature of public buildings, but for good feng shui, you can incorporate a more modest fountain into your home.

Sharp edges cause cutting chi. For good feng shui, ponds, pools, and other water features must be rounded, kidney-shaped, or curved.

IMPROVING AIR QUALITY

Sweet-smelling country air floods into a house, blowing away the cobwebs and getting the air circulating. Rectangular window shapes bring in the good luck chi.

CLEAN, FRESH AIR flowing through your home is important to health. One of the best ways of letting fresh air into the home—and circulating it—is to ventilate the home naturally by opening windows, especially on crisp, sunny, and windy days. Our grandmothers used to open bedroom windows every morning to "air" the room and hang bedding out of the window—a traditional and thrifty custom that's well worth revising.

But many homes today are virtually sealed units. Opening the window for adequate airing or ventilation is not always feasible, and much double or triple glazing is not designed for opening, although if you are installing double-glazing, try to make sure some windows can be opened. The outside air may be polluted, so you need to concentrate on making sure the air quality is pure within your home.

Poor or polluted air in the home can cause colds, headaches, ear, nose, and throat infections,

An ionizer can help to alleviate allergies by reducing the amount of impurities in the air.

If a room does not have a window, use an exhaust fan to preserve air quality.

Re-opening an old fireplace may give your house an alternative form of ventilation and allow it to breathe.

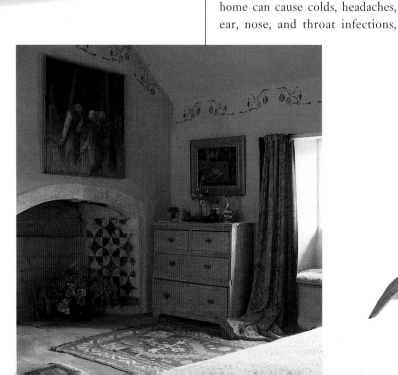

asthma, or allergic reactions. These can be intensified if you undertake large-scale redecoration and structural alterations, which stir up dust and other pollutants.

If you or any of your family are suffering from poor air quality, you can have the air in your home tested professionally by various organizations who will advise on appropriate health measures.

You can also take some simple precautions. If yours is an old house, which originally had an open fireplace and chimneys that have been sealed up, you can

You can test the humidity (percentage of moisture in the air) in your home with a special instrument called an hydrometer. The ideal humidity for a healthy home is 50 to 55 percent. (By contrast, humidity in a desert is 20–25 percent; in a tropical rain forest as high as 95 percent.)

A house plant will renew oxygen levels in the air.

improve air circulation by reopening the fireplace and the chimney, putting a cowl on the top to prevent downdrafts.

You can test for humidity and air purity yourself and then introduce purifiers and humidifiers as needed. If the air in your home is too dry, you will need a humidifier to introduce some moisture. Nonelectric versions can be hung over a radiator and should be filled daily with water; you can add scented aromatherapy oil to enhance the effect. Electric versions produce steam; ultrasonic versions produce a cold vapor; fan-assisted versions can be used in large areas but produce an annoying noise.

Excessive moisture shows itself in condensation on the inside of windows, water on sills, peeling wallpaper, and mold. If dampness is a problem, invest in a dehumidifier. These run on electricity and extract moisture from the atmosphere; some models are combined with a built-in heater.

If pollutants are a problem, you obviously need to try to remove them, but you can also use air purifiers in the home, or try an ionizer, which will suck up tobacco smoke, cooking smells or traffic fumes, pollens, house dust mites, and so on. An ionizer does not have a filter, so it is less efficient than air purifiers, which trap pollutants in an internal filter.

Hoods placed over a stove absorb cooking smells. Some contain a carbon liner that has to be changed regularly; others are

fan-assisted, but are often noisy and can create drafts. Exhaust fans installed in an outside wall or a window, which can be either electrically or hand operated, are another simple means of circulating purer air within the home. Air bricks, too, are another form of ventilation.

House plants can also help to improve the environment by increasing oxygen in the atmosphere, acting as humidifiers and even filtering the air. The popular spider plant, for instance, actually removes formaldehyde and other pollutants from the atmosphere.

AIR CONDITIONING Most

public buildings and an increasing number of homes have air conditioning systems. These control both temperature and humidity and have a very positive role to play. But they can contribute to what is known as sick building syndrome, causing cold-like symptoms when the air is too damp and breathing difficulties when the air is too dry. When you are installing air conditioning, make sure it can both humidify and rehumidify, adding moisture back into the air to prevent it from becoming too dry. Make sure, too, that there is adequate ventilation so that the system circulates fresh rather than stale air. If installing a wet air conditioning system, a closed system that uses water as a coolant, have it professionally cleaned and monitored regularly to keep water from becoming polluted with harmful bacteria or viruses.

SCENTS
FOR
HEALTH

The aromas present in your home establish a welcoming or an uncomfortable atmosphere. Strong foods, such as cabbage, garlic, and fish, or tobacco smoke, can produce unpleasant and overwhelming odors.

REALTORS TELL us if a good, appetizing smell assails our nostrils the moment the front door is opened, it is one of the surest ways of attracting a would-be buyer. The smell of freshly baking bread or cakes, homemade soup on the stove, or coffee brewing all suggest a real home with the kitchen at its center. But some food and other smells are an obvious turn-off—cabbage, cauliflower, stale cooking oil, and of course stale tobacco fumes.

How your home smells will affect how comfortable you feel in it and how welcoming it is for you and others. The sense of smell is controlled by a primitive part of the brain, which is closely connected to the area that also controls mood, emotion, and personality. It also plays a key role in sexual attraction. But these days our sense of smell is becoming eroded, partly because we are forced to inhale

The aromas of bread baking and freshly brewed coffee make any environment seem homely.

Long, heavy curtains can act like a trap, holding onto dust particles, cigarette smoke and cooking smells.

Many household cleaning products have toxic fumes and should be used with care in a ventilated area.

Essential oils are distilled from flowers, woods, and herbs. Heated, they subtly perfume a room.

many unpleasant and toxic smells, such as traffic fumes, plastics, paint solvents, or tobacco smoke. Many commonly used products, too, such as cosmetics, deodorants, air fresheners, detergents, and disinfectants, are highly scented. And even some natural products such as rubber flooring or wood resins can give off an unpleasant or allergy-provoking smell.

We can recover or improve our sense of smell by spending as much time as possible outdoors in clean air, breathing deeply and clearing our lungs. But by making our homes smell more pleasant and natural, we can also improve our sense of smell and, with it, our sense of taste.

There are many ways of improving or enhancing the atmosphere in your home. Some are preventative and involve removing or reducing unpleasant smells and their source; others involve introducing natural scents into the home. Some smells last longer than others, so you need to make sure of adequate ventilation and use extractor systems or air purifiers to make your home smell naturally sweeter. You can also help to prevent food smells from lingering by being careful about the materials you use in your home. Don't use heavy velvet drapes, fabric-covered walls and tented ceilings, thick carpets and rugs, or upholstery in dining or eating areas where they will absorb odors. Similarly, kitchen surfaces should not be absorbent—ceramic tiles or gloss paints are therefore recommended for walls. And take

particular care with open-plan areas, especially where the kitchen is an integral part of the living space.

Improve the smell of your home with natural products: flowers, herbs, and essential oils. Avoid artificial fresheners, particularly spray or aerosol products. Not only do they smell unpleasant but also they are user-unfriendly. Many are more polluting than dust and, if packed in aerosol cans, rely on chlorofluo-rocarbons (CFCs) as a propellant; these are now known to contribute to depletion of the ozone layer.

AROMATHERAPY

Good scents not only improve air quality but also have specific therapeutic qualities. Treating or improving health with essential oils, herbs, and flower extracts is an ancient practice; much traditional medicine in ancient Tibet, China, India, and the Middle East was based almost entirely on the use of aromatic substances. In recent years, aromatherapy has re-emerged as an increasingly popular way of dealing with ailments. Aromatherapy makes use of essential oils, derived from flowers, plants, trees, and resins. Oils can be burned, put in baths, and diluted and placed or massaged on the body. Each essence has different properties that act on the body and mind, influencing the emotions and physical well-being.

Breathing for health
Good breathing encourages health. Far too many people only breathe shallowly through the mouth, instead of using nose, mouth, diaphragm muscles, and lungs to full potential. Many therapies, religions, and philosophies, such as yoga, teach the importance of breathing to bring more oxygen into the blood. Posture is an important aid to proper breathing, and should be applied to sitting, working, and sleeping as well as standing and walking.

Scented flowers and plants act as a natural air freshener. If not overwhelmed by stronger odors, cut flowers can perfume a room for several days.

ENHANCING YOUR HOME

These pages give advice on simple ways of improving air quality and introducing natural fragrances into the home.

• Air rooms daily by opening windows and doors or using exhaust fans, especially in the bathroom and kitchen.

• Make your home a no-smoking zone, or set aside one room for smokers that can be aired easily. Alternatively, banish smokers to the backyard with an ashtray.

• Remove all synthetic materials from your home—plastics, nylon, vinyl, laminates, composite board—and replace them with natural woods, cottons, and other natural materials.

• Use natural materials such as scented beeswax for cleaning and polishing wooden furniture. Beeswax candles also produce a marvelous scent.

• To remove cooking smells, boil pieces of orange, lemon, or lime peel, cinnamon sticks, or cloves in a small saucepan of water. Keep the kitchen well ventilated and close doors while cooking cauliflower or other strong-smelling vegetables. A piece of stale bread in the cooking water or steamer will help to absorb smells.

• Burn scented candles, joss sticks, smudge sticks, incense, or scented oils in pottery burners. Use scented lamp oil. Sprinkle a few drops of oil onto a light bulb or vaporizer ring to permeate the air with a mood-enhancing fragrance.

• Add drops of scented oil to humidifiers or bowls of fresh, tepid water to freshen the air and keep it humid. Change the water daily. Float scented candles in bowls of water, especially when family or friends gather.

• Hang sweet-smelling flowers or bunches of herbs in the kitchen or dining room. Bay leaves, rosemary, sage, lavender, and bergamot smell particularly delicious. Hang dried herbs in cupboards or use them to make potpourri or herb pillows.

• Place fresh flowers throughout the home—an inexpensive way of introducing natural scents. Pot bulbs such as hyacinths or lilies in the fall; as their flowers open in spring, their scent will fill the rooms. Make posies from bay, sage, rosemary, lavender, orange blossom, and mimosa for bedrooms and bathrooms. Also use freesias, arguably the sweetest-smelling flowers of all.

• Fill dishes with potpourri and with a few dried culinary herbs, whole cloves, and cinnamon sticks or bark.

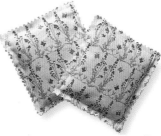

• Store clothes in cedar-lined chests and drawers, leaving doors and drawers slightly open. Use little lavender or herb bags, cakes of naturally scented soaps or pomanders to keep drawers, and your clothes, sweet-smelling. Discourage moths by hanging bunches of fresh or dried bay or rosemary leaves in closets, and strips of dried orange peel, allspice berries, or cedar chips in drawers.

MAKING A
POMANDER Use an orange, lemon, grapefruit, or other citrus fruit. Prick the skin all over with a sharp needle and stud the skin with cloves. Place the fruit in a bag of powdered cinnamon and orris root and shake until well coated. Store in loosely wrapped acid-free tissue paper for about two weeks, attach a ribbon, and hang in a closet.

HERB BAGS
AND PILLOWS Herb pillows, filled with peppermint, spearmint, and eau-de-cologne mint or bergamot, promote healthy sleep, calm the nerves, and can soothe away headaches caused by the stresses of a hectic day.

Hop pillows are also good for insomniacs or those who suffer from asthma—you can sprinkle the hop cones with a little vodka before putting them in the bag.

To make your own pillow or bag, use closely woven gauze or cheesecloth. Cut it to the required size and shape and sew around three sides. Stuff the bag full with crumbled or dried herbs—not powdered—and sew up the fourth side. For sleep pillows, add a few drops of rose or lavender oil to stop the herbs from crackling. Make an outer covering from silk, cotton, or linen. Trim and decorate.

MAKING YOUR OWN
POTPOURRI Potpourri is made from sweet-smelling dried flower petals, aromatic herbs, seeds, and spices. You can also add wood shavings, pine cones, cinnamon sticks, and other "woody" textures. A fixative is necessary to preserve the fragrance, and you can add extra essential oils, but take care not to overdo them, or there will be too many conflicting smells.

Gather flower petals on dry, windless days. Include some buds and small bright flowers for color. Spread the mixture on paper and dry it in a shaded, airy room. Traditionally, strong-smelling rose petals are used, but almost any sweet-scented flowers and herbs can be dried: violets, jasmine, lily of the valley, marigolds, larkspur, pinks, sage, rosemary, bergamot, lavender, lemon verbena, and chamomile, even the gray-leaved curry plant.

Once flowers are dry, mix them in a bowl and add a fixative of orris root or gum benzoin. If you wish add crushed or ground spices—cinnamon, cilantro, nutmeg, cloves, allspice, mace, or anise—or leave them whole for a more robust texture. Use 1 tablespoon of fixative to 5 cups of petals. Mix together and leave in shallow bowls to scent the air.

To make a moist potpourri, do not dry the flower petals. Instead, spread a layer of petals (usually rose) 4 inches deep in an earthenware dish. Cover with a thin layer of salt, add another layer of petals, then salt, and so on until the jar is full. Cover and leave in a dark, airy place for 10–14 days. Stir the mixture with a wooden spoon, add dried orange peel, crushed cloves, and orrisroot. Blend and leave sealed and covered for about five to six weeks. Add a few drops of essential oil, reseal for a further two weeks, then decant into small china or pottery jars.

Add a few drops of pine, lavender, rosemary, or sage oil with a handful of sea salt to a bath for a relaxing end to a busy day.

ESSENTIAL INGREDIENTS

The ceiling of this bedroom is a feature of its architecture—painting it red further enhances the sense of passion in the room.

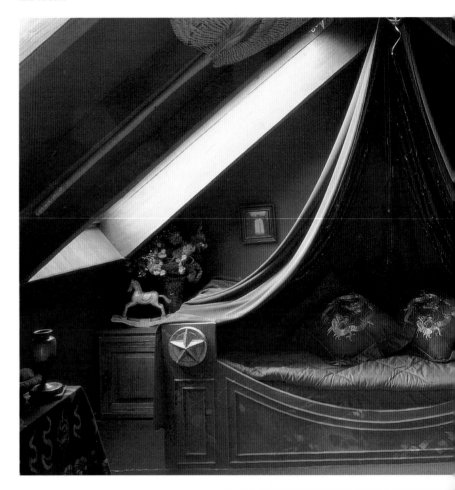

FOR RELAXATION and intimacy, create a sensuous bedroom. It can be a pleasure to share with a partner or to enjoy on your own.

Choose relaxing colors. Blue is calming, green refreshing, but both are cool, so add warmer neutrals such as creams, beiges, taupes, possibly "spiced up" with cinnamon. For a minimalist look, consider cool grays, with light-reflecting textures.

Introduce a little red as a symbol of passion—use heart-shaped pillows, or thread red ribbon through the trimming on a duvet, or pillowcases. Use rich red mounts for a group of prints or introduce red lamp bases.

If red is too strong, consider pink. Use it for walls and ceiling, or for bedhead wall or carpet only. Lilac is a romantic color and can create a sophisticated scheme. Combined with subtle grays, deeper mauves, pinks, and white, lilac is mysterious and elegant.

Peach and terracotta tones will create a warm and intimate ambience. Use paler versions for main surfaces—pale peach ceiling, deeper tones on walls, and a terracotta carpet—combine with refreshing cream and green contrasts.

All too often ceilings are painted "safe" white, yet bedroom and bathroom ceilings are the most noticed ceilings in the home. For a really decorative effect, use a cloudscape, or carry wallpaper up over the ceiling.

If your bedroom is fairly small, choose curtain colors to blend with the wall and relate the color or pattern of the bedding to the flooring. Keep patterns fluid and softly

defined; curved shapes are a good choice—avoid bold geometrics. Keep patterned fabrics for curtains, drapes, and bedding.

Tactile textures are a must and can include strokeable surfaces such as satin, velvet, silk, and fur. Team with gauze and voile for bed drapes and light-diffusing curtains. Soften flooring with exotic rugs, especially by the bed.

Avoid angular furniture—rounded or chamfered corners are much more pleasing—and choose a curvy shape for bed frame or head- and footboards. If you have a rectangular divan, hang bed

Fresh flowers, especially if deliciously scented, will stimulate the senses. Flowers also make a good subject for bedroom pictures.

drapes from a central coronet above the head end, with flowing fabric to each side, held in position with decorative curtain bosses. A serpentine-backed chaise lounge will introduce an attractive form, but if space is limited, use a softly rounded chair with a circular lamp and table.

The use of mirrors in bedrooms should be carefully considered. The mirrored ceiling is out. Mirrored closet doors maximize light and space but should not reflect the bed or too much of the room. For good feng shui, closet mirrors should be covered at night, and mirrors should be circular, oval, or heart-shaped.

Lighting should be soft and romantic, even in the daytime. For drapes, use delicate light-filtering sheer fabric, such as voile, or lace. For a modern look, try slatted blinds. Plan after-dark lighting carefully; install several circuits so you can dim task lighting, and enclose

pendant light bulbs in a suitable shade. Soft-glow uplighters or wall washers give off a gentle light.

For an aura of mystery, conceal a floor-mounted uplighter behind a large "sculptural" plant, in among flowers or a group of plants, or behind a screen. This will create attractive shadows. Kinetic lighting is the most magical—glowing candles give a soft, flattering light. Nothing is more wonderful than the flicker of firelight, so if you have a chimney in the room, consider installing an open fire.

Bedrooms should also smell enticing—though you should avoid a heavy scent! The smell of fresh air and newly washed linen may be all that is needed, or a posy of sweet-smelling flowers. You can create stronger scents by burning scented oils or joss sticks.

Choose pictures for the bedroom with care. Avoid abstracts or disturbing scenes in favor of floral prints or landscape paintings. Feng shui advises against pictures of solitary people or stark settings.

Adding textiles to a bedroom that you automatically want to run your hand across—such as these embroidered lace cushions—introduces the sensuousness of touch to the room (far left).

Softly draped fabrics help to diffuse light in the bedroom, while neutral creams create a relaxed mood (left).

THINGS

really healthy home needs living things in
the form of plants, flowers, and possibly
animals. Plants encourage physical and
emotional well-being; carefully chosen and nur-
tured, they provide a refreshing environment in
which you can relax and enjoy a link with the
natural world. Indoors, healthy plants, whether
purchased houseplants or plants you have grown
yourself, can be incorporated into your environment to create a mini-ecosystem, which supplies
oxygen and helps to control humidity. An outdoor
green space, even if it is only a modest patio, provides somewhere to sit calmly away from everyday
worries and contemplate nature.

In ideal way of creating a peaceful green space
might be a be a plant-filled sunroom leading onto
a sheltered patio, which provides visual links to a
garden beyond. The yard itself can be designed to
create a group of outdoor "rooms," complete with
arbors, gazebos, summerhouses, and water features. You can build a simple bower, with fragrant
climbing shrubs sheltering a seat, which can be
"upholstered" with herbs such as chamomile or
thyme, and surrounded by scented flowers and
herbs. Such a scented corner would be much
appreciated by the partially sighted and also by
the elderly, but can provide a place of peaceful soli-
tude for anyone.

In you live in an apartment, or a house with
only a tiny backyard, you can still bring color,
greenery, and nature into your home. Put plants
in pots outside your front and back doors or in
hanging baskets indoors; windowboxes on outside
sills; herbs and potted plants on indoor windowsills;
shrubs, plants, and flowers on balconies; fresh
flowers in vases throughout the house. If you have
a particularly sunny windowsill, you can stretch
glazed shelves across it and use them to grow a
selection of plants, herbs, and flowers that will trail
attractively down and climb upward.

Even if your apartment lacks windowsills or balconies and is situated up several flights of stairs,
you can still place shrubs such as a bay tree outside
the entrance door if the hall is well lit, or plant a
large glass jar to create a tiny garden in a bottle.

Virtually every room in your home will benefit
from houseplants: water-loving plants in the bathroom, herbs and other scented plants in the
kitchen, romantically soft-colored and scented
plants in the bedroom, and dramatically shaped
plants for empty corners, or where you want to
create the illusion of greater height. And you can
use lamps, spotlighting, and mirrors to dramatize
their presence and increase the sense of well-being
that plants provide.

Animals, too, can play a part in creating a healthy
home. Pets, particularly cats and dogs, are known
to have a therapeutic role in combating stress.
Snakes, iguanas, and other reptiles can bring fasci-
nation into the home, and, if such animals are not
appealing to you, you can maintain an aquarium
full of fish for a colorful and therapeutic effect.

USING HOUSEPLANTS

IF YOUR HOME has no garden, sunroom, or greenhouse, and you haven't the time to grow your own plants, then houseplants are a most effective way of bringing greenery and nature into the home. There is a huge choice of houseplants available today, from modest African violets to highly exotic species, and many can be obtained from garden centers, supermarkets, and even your local convenience store. As their name suggests, houseplants are grown for use indoors; properly cared for, they can survive for years.

Houseplants can be chosen purely for their beauty and to add decorative visual elements to the home, but they also encourage health and reduce toxicity. During the daytime, through the process of photosynthesis, plants absorb harmful carbon dioxide and other impurities from the atmosphere and release health-giving oxygen. They also take in water from soil and let it out through their leaves, which helps maintain the proper humidity levels in the home. To maximize this effect, it is a good idea to group plants rather than place them individually.

PLACEMENT Healthy plants reflect a healthy environment. Although houseplants are sold for indoor use, the home is not a natural environment for plants, so you need to create exactly the right conditions for them to thrive. Some plants, such as cacti, need dry conditions; others, such as African violets, thrive in a moist atmosphere and are ideal for bathrooms. A few, such as ivy, tolerate shade. Their needs will therefore influence which plants you choose for the various rooms in your home.

In a way, plants are also living accessories that you incorporate into the overall design of your home. You can group them for maximum impact, or stand them singly to fill a gap. Size, form, color, and texture are therefore important and need to be considered in relation to the space available and the decor of your rooms. Tall sculptural plants will look good in a large space; smaller, more compact plants will sit happily on a windowsill; trailing plants can be used to soften sharp corners and look particularly effective on shelves. Frondy plants can be trained to grow up walls in your home, supported on sticks or trellis.

Wherever you decide to place your plants, check that light and temperature levels are adequate for their needs. If light is limited, you may want to use special daylight bulbs to encourage growth. Be flexible in your planning, and move

Plants and health

It has been known for some time that houseplants are good for your health. They freshen the atmosphere, filter dust and other particles from the environment, and some actually absorb pollutants such as tobacco smoke, solvent fumes, and formaldehyde. Various plants such as peace lilies and philodendron can even counteract the effects of electromagnetic radiation emitted by computers, televisions, and microwaves. So impressive are their effects that the American space agency, NASA, which has done considerable research into their antipolluting qualities, has used plants on board manned space vehicles and space stations to purify and refresh the air.

Antipolluting plants:

Potted chrysanthemums

Spider plant (Chlorophytum variegatum)

Aspidistra lurida

Mother-in-law's tongue (Sansevieria laurentii)

Gerbera daisies

Devil's ivy (Scindapsus aureus)

Variegated ivies (Hedera helix & Hedera canariensis)

Sweetheart plant (Philodendron scandens) [antiradiation]

Peace lilies (Spathiphyllum wallissii) [antiradiation]

Whatever the environment in your room—shady, full sun, very dry, or high humidity—there is a houseplant that can thrive in it.

plants around sometimes to give them a little vacation and change of scene—they will benefit from this just as much as you do! Your plants may also need feeding with special liquid fertilizer, and dead-heading—removing dead flowers or leaves. Light and water are essential for growth, but check that you do not overwater your plants—a very common fault. Research their needs, and follow cultivation instructions. Some plants, such as cyclamens or poinsettias prefer near-dry soil; others need daily watering. It is best to stand pots in water and let plants absorb what they need through their roots, but never leave them standing in too much water. In nature plants are watered from above, which washes their leaves; you may therefore need to spray houseplants from time to time.

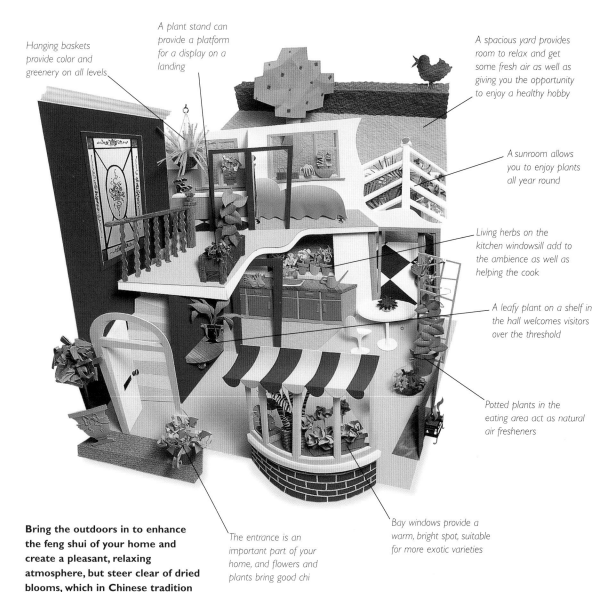

A plant stand can provide a platform for a display on a landing

Hanging baskets provide color and greenery on all levels

A spacious yard provides room to relax and get some fresh air as well as giving you the opportunity to enjoy a healthy hobby

A sunroom allows you to enjoy plants all year round

Living herbs on the kitchen windowsill add to the ambience as well as helping the cook

A leafy plant on a shelf in the hall welcomes visitors over the threshold

Potted plants in the eating area act as natural air fresheners

Bay windows provide a warm, bright spot, suitable for more exotic varieties

The entrance is an important part of your home, and flowers and plants bring good chi

Bring the outdoors in to enhance the feng shui of your home and create a pleasant, relaxing atmosphere, but steer clear of dried blooms, which in Chinese tradition spell bad luck. Opt for silk plants or flowers if fresh flowers and plants are out of the question.

BRINGING THE OUTSIDE IN

ONE OF THE FINEST ways to relax, reduce tension, and de-stress yourself is to work with flowers and green plants, whether or not you have a green thumb. Handling earth and seedlings, which you may have grown from the original seed, pricking out, potting, taking cuttings, pruning, and then enjoying the fruits of your labors are very therapeutic. If you have time and space, growing your own plants for indoor use is enormously satisfying. And if you have a garden, sunroom, or greenhouse, there are endless design possibilities.

Another advantage of growing your own plants, or propagating them from existing plants, is that they will tolerate your home environment more easily than purchased plants. You can also give cuttings away to friends and family, who will return the compliment.

Plants bring health into the home, but can also be combined with accessories and furniture to help create a specific design style— an aspidistra in a decorative cache pot placed on a wooden or cast-iron aspidistra stand surrounded by ferns creates a late-19th-century feel; neatly shaped bonsai trees set in shallow containers are oriental in flavor; cacti and succulents mulched with sand or fine gravel look eclectic; beautifully arranged cut flowers, or containers filled with flowering bulbs or corms, such as lilies, hyacinths, freesias, or cyclamen, evoke an English country house; while posies of wildflowers and herbs suggest a simple cottage style.

However, you do need to create the right conditions for plants to grow and flourish; they need light, humidity, the right type of potting soil, and occasional feeding, as well as water. If you have a porch built for plants, a sunroom, or even an atrium created by glazed walls or a roof of "lantern" light, it should not be too difficult to provide the right conditions and produce a healthy selection of indoor plants, providing a visual link to the outside. You can also grow more unusual items such as citrus trees, indoor vines and exotic vegetables.

Improvise if your home does not include a greenhouse or sunroom. For instance, if you have a particularly sunny window, you can build a simple mini-greenhouse out of wood and glass and attach it to the outside frame. Place shelves inside the structure to hold

There is a great deal of satisfaction to be gained from growing your own flowers and then bringing them into the home to brighten a room.

If you don't have a garden, you can still grow plants on a windowsill. A scented herb garden will provide pleasure and a useful product.

plants and seedlings, which will grow just as well as in a full-size greenhouse. Remember, however, plants will need some screening from sun and frost. You could build a similar structure on a small outside balcony, or inside a bay window; alternatively, you could glass in a small balcony to create a mini-greenhouse or sunroom.

Use any sunny windowsill in your home to display or grow herbs and plants, some trailing down, others growing upward. You can place glass shelves across the window, and mount pots on them, bearing in mind the need to protect them from scorching in direct sunlight. A stained-glass panel behind the pots can look very dramatic, and you can use concealed lighting to create even

more impact. This can also be a successful way of screening an overlooked window, or of bringing some greenery into a poorly lit basement. In this case, you will need plants such as ivy or ferns that do not need too much light to flourish.

If light allows, the kitchen is a wonderful place to grow herbs such as chives, parsley, sweet basil, and scented-leaved geraniums. Pansies, violas, pot marigolds, and nasturtiums will also look good.

You could combine any of these plants with miniature tomato plants—there are some tumbling varieties that look particularly decorative—or small chili or pepper plants. All these plants will add to the decorative quality of the meal that you serve: a green salad

garnished with chive flowers and violas; a dish of grilled vegetables with oregano, marigold, and nasturtium flowers; a summer dessert trimmed with appropriate soft fruits, pansy flowers, and apple mint will all look wonderfully appetizing on the table.

You can use hanging baskets and windowboxes inside the home. Fill baskets with trailing indoor plants and hang them on hooks, or position windowboxes on brackets, planting them with trailing plants or flowers. Line windowboxes carefully, support them on a drip tray to avoid staining walls, and take them down when watering or feeding plants. Alternatively, plant in separate pots and use the windowbox or a jardiniere to hide pots from view. Fill the box with pebbles to increase humidity but prevent the roots from becoming drenched.

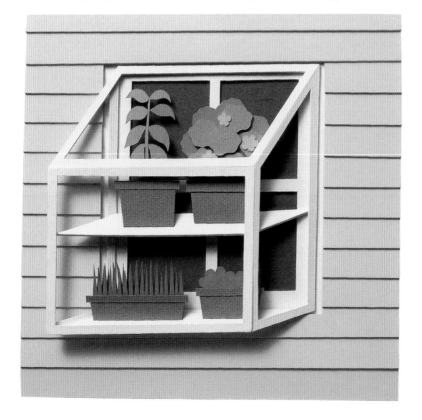

RECYCLING CONTAINERS

You can grow plants in almost anything, including old milk churns and water-bath canners.

PLANT CONTAINERS lend themselves to recycling and, depending on what they are, can be used both indoors and out. I devised a very successful indoor herb and plant arrangement for a kitchen, using a recycled 7-tier saucepan stand, which held plants in different-sized pots. The feet of the stand stood in a deep circular tray, and I watered the plants from the top so the water flowed down through the pots and was collected in the tray. The effect was stylish, filled an empty corner, was virtually troublefree, and enabled me to recycle an old possession.

Be creative with containers. A small strawberry or parsley pot with little "pockets" looks very effective filled with different herbs such as thyme, oregano, chervil, tarragon, lemon verbena, or purple basil, topped with a tumbling miniature tomato. The old-fashioned pitcher and bowl set from a washstand can be used for an unusual spring indoor garden with various green plants trailing down around the edge and the center

filled with pots of spring bulbs—crocus, hyacinths, narcissus, and daffodils. I keep the arrangement fairly low by using short miniature bulbs; the pitcher is filled with water and cut evergreens to add height, and placed beside the bowl on an old washstand.

Old jugs, teapots, bowls, bread boxes, and vegetable dishes can all be used as decorative containers, as can metal churns, enamel pitchers, old pots, and saucepans, if they are attractive. If you are going to place plant and soil directly into these containers, they will need adequate drainage. Drill holes in the bottom of the container and then fill the base with gravel or pieces of old terracotta flowerpots to allow water to drain and perhaps a few lumps of charcoal to keep the soil sweet.

Old china or earthenware sinks, or handbasins without pedestals make very successful recycled containers. They are extremely heavy to transport, but have the advantage of built-in drainage. Even so, they need to be filled with broken pots and gravel for good drainage, and to be supported on solid wood or bricks. Although these are mostly used as outdoor displays, they can be very effective in a sunroom, large hall, or dining room.

Old fish tanks or an aquarium can be filled with colored gravel or sand and used to grow a selection of cacti. A round goldfish bowl can be similarly adapted, but might be best with one plant only. Wide-mouthed glass jars with interesting shapes and unusual colors can also be used as planters. Different

Recycle imaginatively. Bright yellow marigolds look quite striking growing out of a pair of old boots.

An old claw-foot bath, filled with dahlia and lobelia, makes a colorful patio display.

shaped bottles, grouped together and filled with plants, can look stunning, especially if the arrangement is lit with accent lighting at night.

Birdcages, whether circular Chinese-style, delicate late-19th-century metal varieties, or made of bamboo and cane, also make decorative plant containers. All can be filled with trailing houseplants or feathery ferns, hung by the side of a window or from a sunroom roof. Many wire containers such as salad shakers or stacks of wire trays take on a totally new look when filled with plants.

Old tubs can be used successfully as plant containers on a patio and in sunrooms, as can old horse troughs. A metal primer and coats of colorful paint will help to

protect containers from the elements. You could use green to fade the container into the environment, or make it a feature with rich or exciting colors. Other possibilities include sewing-machine stands and recycled farm machinery. Any of

Gardening allows everyone to be creative. Designing your own containers brings enormous satisfaction.

these can form a distinctive garden grouping that is more original than the classic pieces of statuary that are readily obtainable from stores.

Reclaimed earthenware conduit pipes can also look very decorative used as containers—you can stand a second plant pot inside the rim, or balance a half-circle wire basket on top and plant it with trailing plants. Such pipes can also be incorporated into water features providing attractive and unusual ways of routing the flow. Salvaged bricks can be recycled to build attractive raised beds in the garden or on a patio. They can also be used for standing containers on to create different levels in the garden.

TERRARIUMS Named after the 19th-century botanist Dr. Nathaniel Ward, who invented them, terrariums are tiny enclosed gardens, ideal for indoor use and slow-growing plants. A sealed terrarium will effectively create its own microclimate, cycling and recycling all the plants' needs inside the glass container. Water in the soil is taken up by the plants and released through the leaves. Moisture then condenses onto the glass top and sides, running back into the soil. As a result, a terrarium only needs watering about twice a year. The plants inside do not need to be fed since they manufacture all the food they need. For best results, a terrarium should sit in a light, bright position where it receives about 6 or 7 hours light a day, but should not be placed in direct sunlight.

A terrarium is a beautiful self-sustaining garden in miniature, ideal for indoors. Place it in a light position, out of direct sun.

HEALTHY PLANTS and freshly cut flowers bring good feng shui into the home. They enhance energy flows, offset stagnation, improve air quality, and can be used to solve various problems.

The color and type of plant or flower you choose will be in tune with the theory of the five elements and will enhance the element you need. Cut flowers kept in clear water bring invigorating energies into the home, but both flowers and water must be kept fresh; stagnant water is poor feng shui, and wilting or dying flowers mean bad luck and will have a negative effect on energy. Artificial flowers, particularly those made of natural materials such as silk or paper, are always preferable to wilting plants and can be used as symbolic cures.

Flower containers also have symbolic meaning. Clear glass vases in curved shapes add a tranquil water chi energy; metal containers help to enhance the metal chi energy, which is good for romance, style, and finance. Silver or red will increase the effect, but the color of flowers should be carefully related to their container. Tall streamlined wooden containers are associated with uplifting tree energy; pyramid shapes increase fire energy; and low bowls or troughs, perhaps containing floating flower heads and candles, are associated with family harmony. Square containers are associated with the earth element.

Plants must be kept absolutely healthy for good feng shui. The overall size and shape of a plant and the shape of its leaves will help to create different effects. Tall plants will generate more tree chi energy, and if they have pointed or star-shaped leaves, they will help to move chi energy more quickly; they should not, however, be used in small rooms. Round-leafed plants calm energy flow and can be used to soften dangerous sharp corners in a house and counteract cutting chi. Low, bushy plants help to slow down fast-moving chi energy, so are ideal placed in long, narrow halls and corridors or near doors; trailing plants are, like waterfalls, associated with water energy.

It is best to group plants together, using a variety of different shapes and types; their different qualities will complement and balance each other, and provide a better flow of chi energy. The position of some plants must be chosen with care. Plants with thorns or spiky leaves such as yuccas, cacti, or palms give off a spiky energy; they should not be positioned too close to a seating area or bed. Feng Shui practitioners believe that their energy can provide a security

Red flowers boost fire energy, linked to passion and good luck.

White flowers boost metal energy; tall stems carry wood energy.

device so they are best placed in enclosed porches to ward off any potential threat.

In areas that lack natural light such as internal bathrooms, rooms overshadowed by trees or buildings, or a basement, plants can help to increase chi energy, freshen air, and increase humidity. It is difficult to find plants that will thrive in dark conditions, so use special daylight bulbs to encourage growth, or stand plants on a sheet of mirror glass or place a mirror behind them to increase any natural daylight. For these conditions, choose plants like ivy (*Hedera helix*) and ferns, which will tolerate shady conditions. As they are associated with water in feng shui, they are particularly appropriate in a bathroom.

Plants can also be used to help improve the problem of low, or sloping ceilings; tall plants, such as palms, aspidistras, or fig trees (*Ficus*), placed in strategic positions, will help to keep energy flowing upward and away from the area below the slope, and palms are ideal in the corners. If you combine these with uplighters, hidden among the base of the plants, light will be thrown up onto the ceiling, also helping to improve the upward flow.

Plants can be used to soften protruding corners or the sharp corners on furniture and shelves. You can trail a bushy plant down or up to cover the corner and control cutting chi. For this solution, choose a plant with rounded leaves like the philodendron, tradescantia, or ficus. And if you have awkward internal corners, plants with long, sharp pointed leaves, such as palms, spider plants (*Chlorophytum*), yucca, or dracaena (*Dracaena marginata*) will prevent stagnation and get the chi energy circulating.

If you have long corridors or narrow dark halls, stagger plants on either side, to slow down the fast-moving chi. This cure also works well with plants in pots placed down a narrow path outside the front door. Plants in a porch or on either side of the front door create a feeling of welcome and well-being, and can be enjoyed as you go out and come home.

Because houseplants help to counteract the effects of electrical radiation from home appliances, feng shui suggests putting indoor plants between the source of radiation and where you want to relax, or in the center of the house. A peace lily is particularly effective.

In the kitchen, plants will add natural, living energy to the food preparation and storage areas. Tall plants will add tree chi energy, which is harmonious with water and fire. In the bathroom, tall plants help to drain excess water energy.

Yellowish squat flowers like marigolds boost earth energy.

Blue ground-covering plants such as aubretia enhance water energy.

SUNROOMS AND GREENHOUSES

IF YOU ARE LUCKY enough to have the space—and the budget—a sunroom can be a wonderful extension to a healthy home. It can give you extra living space since it may well be used in summer as a dining or living room, provide a place for indoor gardening, and give you a green center with a calm, soothing, and refreshing ambience where you can reduce tension and restore shattered nerves.

In the 18th and 19th centuries, sunrooms were used as camellia houses or orangeries or to plant unusual plants brought back by intrepid botanists from trips overseas. Today you can use your sunroom to grow exotic plants, indoor vines, unusual fruit and vegetables, and possibly introduce a soothing water feature.

Followers of feng shui will need to call in a consultant before embarking on a sunroom project, because adding a structure to your home will affect energy flows and the natural balance of the environment. But even those who do not practice feng shui may choose to call in experts, who will advise on ventilation, watering, and screening systems as well as choice of plants. They will also be able to advise on lighting and heating systems, many of which are now self-adjusting.

A sunroom or conservatory can range from a large prefabricated structure, which includes everything from furniture, fixtures, and plants, to a small lean-to greenhouse you build yourself, which can be set against an outside wall and which will provide a small, sheltered green space for you to work with your plants. You can even create a very successful mini-sunroom by glassing in a porch or flat roof.

PLANTING The plants you choose depend on the type of sunroom you want to create. For a "Return to the Raj" type, which was common in the late 19th and early 20th centuries, you could furnish with period pieces—cane, wicker, and a ceiling fan—and plant parlor palms, aspidistras, ferns, and other plants popular at the time.

Alternatively, a conservatory can be planted for all-year color, with flowering plants, shrubs, bulbs, and so on planned to come into bloom at different seasons. Foliage plants will also be important; choose them for color—green, deep red, or bronze; variegated—for their texture and for the color of their flowers. For all-year interest, remember to include some evergreen plants in your arrangement.

Grouping and tactile impact are also important, so aim to use different textures and shapes: tall, treelike shrubs; trailing, feathery ferns; spreading, glossy-leafed varieties; low, compact shapes; and spiky varieties. You might also want to experiment with citrus trees; they look wonderful in pots and may reward you with your own lemons, kumquats, or limes. If you are patient, you can grow these from seeds.

A greenhouse or sunroom lets you enjoy plants all year round. Group them by height and color for interest.

Warmth and luxurious green plants refresh the spirit and calm the nerves. A lean-to greenhouse (below) provides space for growing plants and, if insulated, also traps heat.

Light and healthy green plants encourage good feng shui and are soothing and refreshing. Adding a sunroom (above and right) changes the home's energy balance, so you may want to check positioning with a consultant.

SOLAR GREENHOUSES

Solar systems can also be used to bring on seedlings, grow plants and herbs, and even grow food. A solar greenhouse, which is attached to the house on the sun-facing side, is a different concept from a sunroom, although it can be used similarly for leisure purposes and as an extra room. With adequate thermal insulation, the warmth can be "trapped" and used to heat the area in the evening and to warm water for the plants.

It is also possible to use solar energy to heat a separate greenhouse, warm propagators, and so on. Interestingly, solar greenhouses are related to the 18th-century orangery (and later the "glass house" of the late 19th century).

This was a separate building from the rest of the house, but it had a thick brick back wall, usually on the north side, with a system of chimneys and open fires on the outside, which heated the brick; the rest of the sun-facing walls were glass. In winter, maximum use was made of the sun to keep the temperature suitable for growing citrus fruit, pineapples, vines, and so on, but extra heat was provided by lighting the fires and letting out the warmth slowly. This is another reason why walled gardens were popular—the warmth of the sun retained in the brick on a walled kitchen garden provided ideal growing and ripening facilities for fruit such as peaches and apricots.

GARDENS

A formal herb garden, featuring the beautiful contrast of purple and green sage, complements this gothic summerhouse with trailing wisteria vines.

Box hedge is a traditional border for formal gardens and will provide background greenery all year round.

EVEN THE SMALLEST backyard or tiny town garden can become a beautiful outdoor green space. Don't discount your front yard either, or the strip running along the side of the house; these areas can also be designed and planted for maximum effect.

Before beginning, you need to consider which way your yard faces and the amount of natural light it receives. Soil type, too, is an important consideration. If you have a north- or northeast-facing garden, which is shady for most of the day, look for shade-loving plants or those that thrive in damp conditions. If you have a sunny south- or southwest-facing garden with lots of good drainage and a tendency to dry out when the sun shines, you may find it better to concentrate on creating a Mediterranean-style garden, full of aromatic and tactile herbs and plants that thrive in dry conditions and attract wildlife such as birds, bees, and butterflies.

If you want a frankly sensual garden, choose plants for their scent, touch, and visual quality and plan paths to meander among them, so you brush against them as you stroll by. You could plant small cushionlike herbs such as thyme, chamomile, and feverfew between paving stones on a patio or garden path, so the scent is released when you walk on them. Fragrant plants in pots close to a front or back door or window can be enjoyed every time you pass by and can also be placed close to any outside sitting or eating area. If you want to give the patio, terrace, or veranda a Tuscan or French-Riviera flavor, add trellising and grow climbing plants—perhaps even a grapevine—up over it, forming a canopy over the top as a natural screen.

If your garden is fairly small, consider paving most of it, perhaps with one or two raised beds, and use plants in containers to provide greenery, color, and fragrance. One of the advantages of this type of garden is that you can change the planting to suit the season, perhaps filling the edge of pots with spring, summer, or autumn flowers, and planting a more permanent fixture, such as a flowering shrub, in the center. You can also move containers around fairly easily, so any plants that need a little more sun or light can be moved to a better position for a few weeks, giving another group of plants a refreshing vacation in the shade. For good effect, vary the height of plants and containers you choose.

Color is important. Plan for background greenery all year round—this can be provided by evergreens—and use small trees and shrubs that look good in winter, even without foliage. Eucalyptus has wonderful silver-gray stems and foliage; the stems of cornus turn deep red or golden orange in the fall and last right through the winter; the bark of a silver birch tree seen against a clear blue winter sky is a magical sight. Then use colored flowers, plants, and flowering shrubs to create mood or lift your spirits. Red, yellow, orange, purple, and strong pink are dynamic and energizing; green, blue, and

Varying shades of green and soft, muted mauve set against natural paving stones encourage a feeling of calm and restfulness.

Color in the garden creates mood and atmosphere just as it does indoors. Reds, yellows, and purple are active, energizing colors that create a sense of excitement.

If you have the space, plan your yard as a series of outdoor rooms. If space is limited, try adding a feature that suggests there is a room beyond.

white are more calming and low-key. Don't worry about colors clashing; they never do in nature.

If you prefer to be a little more restrained, you could color-grade your plants in flowerbeds or a group of containers. Use yellow and white with rich green and grayish foliage; mix yellow and orange with warm copper-colored leaf plants such as berberis, cornus, or copper beech; show off deep blues and purples against paler mauves and pinks, with subtle gray and silver foliage.

If you are lucky enough to have plenty of space, you might be able to design the whole yard as a series of outdoor rooms: a green room, enclosed by shrubs or neatly clipped hedges as a place to sit and relax; an herb garden, possibly planned in the style of a traditional 16th-century knot garden; a water garden complete with pool and bridge over the stream; a childrens' play area with tree house, jungle gym, swing, and sandpile; an outdoor dining area, complete with table, chairs, and barbecue—the possibilities are endless.

Try also to grow some of your own food. Use a walled area if you have the space, or a series of raised beds. If space is limited, you can place unusual vegetables and fruit-bearing trees among the flowers and plants; miniature versions of these are designed to be grown in pots or hanging baskets, so they can be included on even the smallest patio. Peaches, apricots, plums, apples, and pears can be trained fan- or espalier-fashion against trellising, forming a screen or natural

division between areas, and you will enjoy the fresh fruit at harvest time—there is nothing more wonderful than a fresh peach, fig, or mulberry picked and eaten warm, straight from the tree.

Aim to garden organically, especially if you plan to grow your own fruit and vegetables. Organically grown food is much healthier, and is often tastier, than nonorganic food. Organic gardening will also encourage more wildlife into the garden, with no danger of animals being poisoned by harmful chemicals.

The important thing is to cultivate food in nature's own way in organic soil, which is full of natural minerals, and fed organically as well. One of the best and most inexpensive ways of doing this is

to use compost to mulch and feed the plants. You can make compost either in a traditional compost heap hidden away in a corner or in special composting drums and bins. In a small garden an enclosed container, or a heap covered with black plastic, is more socially acceptable!

Pest control should also be organic. Don't use sprays or insecticides. Instead, encourage wildlife to rid your plants of pests such as aphids. You can even buy some natural predators such as lacewings or ladybugs.

To start you off on your organic garden, buy plants, seeds, and products from established organic suppliers. For a list of recommended sources, see the Useful Addresses section at the end of the book.

Making compost

Most leftover foods—old vegetable peels, tea leaves, coffee grounds, fruit cores and rinds—can be composted into a nourishing fertilizer for the garden. You can also include small scraps of paper, cotton waste, grass cuttings, and fallen leaves.

Use a special container, either homemade or purchased from a garden supplier. These can be made from metal or wood and come in various sizes. Site compost in a handy shaded position, away from playing or dining areas, and screen it from view with trellising, fencing, or plants. Line the container with newspaper, and collect your kitchen waste in a sheet of newspaper or an old paper bag, which can be added to the compost bin. There are several natural ways of activating the breakdown of waste, including using liquid from the comfrey plant, which you can grow for the purpose, or seaweed. Special "wormeries" are available from garden specialists; the worms live on the refuse and speed up the composting process.

Widespread and long-term use of pesticides may be linked to serious disorders such as leukemia. By gardening organically, you avoid introducing harmful pesticides and other chemicals into the food chain and at the same time produce healthy, tasty, and pollutant-free vegetables for eating.

FENG SHUI GARDENS

A feng shui garden aims to provide a calm setting in which to meditate and think. It should echo nature and be as natural-looking as possible. Rocks, for example, are appreciated for their color, texture, and form. Rocks in feng shui gardens are not covered with alpine plants, although grasses and other sculptural plants can be incorporated into the design to enhance the effect of the rocks.

Straight lines should be avoided, and gently curved and S-shaped paths should be designed to meander along, shifting as the view changes. In some traditional mobile feng shui gardens, screens, trellises, and walls are used to create a series of outdoor rooms, so the visitor moves from one experience to another. Bridges over water should curve gently upward to encourage you to look into the water and to contemplate the reflections. A willow, with branches dipping gracefully into the stream, is a powerful water symbol.

No feng shui garden is complete without a water feature. Its surface should be reflective and the shape curvaceous; on a flat site, build an interestingly shaped pond; on a sloping site aim for the more naturalistic look of a gently flowing stream, waterfall, or rivulets. Water must be kept moving, so use a pump to recycle the water. The pump must be silent because the sound of running water is an integral part of the overall effect of the feng shui garden.

A garden planned according to the principles of feng shui should contain a water feature to promote the flow of energy.

LOW-ALLERGEN GARDENS

HAY FEVER, asthma, and allergies to pollen and other air-borne irritants are extremely widespread, and for millions of people who suffer from these conditions, the effects interfere with the pleasure of ordinary gardens or plant life. However, if you or a member of your family suffers from any of these ailments, you can create a special low-allergen garden.

If you have the space, select a suitable site, which should be away from the rest of the garden, or create your whole garden as a low-allergen space using walls, fences, and trellises as alternatives to hedges and shrubs. Design a water feature that will create an atmosphere of peace and calm among the green foliage and plants and keep the air moist.

It is essential to choose the plants carefully. Some evergreen plants and shrubs are low in pollen and are therefore suitable. Flowering plants that are insect-pollinated are more suitable than wind-pollinated flowers because the pollen is heavy and too large to inhale; it is also not blown so widely into the air. Avoid plants with a heavy scent; as an alternative you can use sweet-smelling herbs such as mint, rosemary, or oregano.

If you personally have hay fever, plan and do structural work in your garden during the winter, and plant the garden in early spring when the pollen count is low. During mid-summer, when the pollen count may be high, enjoy or work in your garden in early morning, or on cloudy or cooler days.

Hay fever and other allergies can make outdoor life a misery. By making some simple changes and introducing specialized plants, you can create a low-allergen garden.

Use gravel for mulching

Use paving instead of grass lawns

Avoid rotting vegetation and compost, which release mold spores

Plant low-allergen ground cover to avoid weeds

Replace heavily
scented plants with
lightly fragrant herbs

Choose insect-
pollinated plants

Take out unsuitable
plants and replace with
low-allergen varieties

Remove hedges and
replace with painted
fence or wall

Low-allergen plants

Choose plants that are
insect-pollinated, rather than
wind-pollinated.

Most shrubs are insect-pollinated,
with the exception of ones that
are heavily scented, such as:
*honeysuckle, jasmine, and
philadelphus.*

Most flowers are also insect-
pollinated, but those who are
pollen sensitive should avoid
*asters, carnations, chrysanthemums,
dahlias, daisies, dandelions,
goldenrod, pinks, and sweet william.*

Heavily scented plants that can
also cause a problem include
*daffodils, freesias, hyacinths, roses,
and sweet peas.*

Most trees are wind-pollinated and
should be kept well away from the
house. Particular ones to avoid are
*ash, beech, birch, elder, hazel, horse
chestnut, lime, oak, pine, plane,
poplar, sycamore, willow, and yew.*

Herbs are insect-pollinated, but
pick them before they flower to
avoid any possible allergens.

PETS

Guardians of the home, dogs bring life, energy, and companionship—in feng shui, they are associated with earth energy. For young children, smaller animals, such as rabbits, provide something to cherish.

PETS, especially cats and dogs, are very much an integral part of life in North America, Australia, Great Britain, and some areas of Europe, and are often treated like one of the family. A well-cared-for family pet can help in the emotional development of children, giving them the chance to love and care for something smaller and more helpless than themselves, thereby increasing their awareness of others' needs. A pet can also give a child a safety valve: something to hug, stroke, love, and talk to, which can be very therapeutic. Keeping a pet can also help to teach a child the facts of life as well as preparing them for the natural cycle of life from birth to death.

Children in both town and country have little contact with wild or larger domesticated animals; they may be fortunate enough to visit nearby city farms or a wildlife park, where, however, animals are not always seen in truly natural conditions. And zoos and circuses often give a completely wrong impression of animals, so that keeping a pet is often a child's main contact with the animal world.

Animals and pets can also help reduce stress, both for adults and for teenagers. Many people, especially the elderly, live solitary lives, and a cat or dog can be a comforting friend. Pets welcome their owners when they return home and these living creatures can be talked to and fussed over, possibly preventing their owners from becoming depressed. Stroking and grooming a cat, rabbit, guinea pig, gerbil, hamster, or dog is known to be therapeutic; it relieves tension, reduces the pulse rate, and lowers blood pressure. The work of guide dogs for the blind, partially sighted, and deaf also provides an example of how animals can provide practical help for humans.

Dogs in the house also provide security. They offer a shield, without the need to turn the house into a fortress, particularly for those living alone, because burglars are likely to be deterred by a bark or growl. They also offer protection when walking in city or town streets, or along lonely country lanes. The very fact that a dog needs regular exercise and to be taken for walks encourages its owner to take a healthy walk twice a day, another way of reducing tension and keeping fit.

Walking a dog can also be an antidote to loneliness and a good way of meeting people, particularly if you are new to an area or neighborhood. If you don't want to keep a dog yourself, you could always offer to walk a dog for someone else in your area.

Long-haired cats or dogs can be problematic for those who suffer from asthma or allergies. Short-haired cats, such as Burmese, Siamese, or Abyssinians, can be suitable; they are supremely elegant and can be enjoyed for their feline grace. A more recent breed, which is almost hairless, is the Devon Rex. The sound of a purring cat is extremely soothing and can be a sensuous experience. Some short-haired cats are pedigreed, and must be obtained from

Cats are beautiful to watch. They can help relieve stress and tension, but are predatory creatures.

breeders rather than pet shops, although some mixed breeds have short enough hair to be fairly low-allergen. Some dogs, notably poodles, which have fleece-like fur, are also relatively allergen-free. Special vacuum cleaners with cleaning heads and filters are available to deal with pet hairs, and these will help to control potential breathing problems associated with animal hair.

For those who want animals in the house but do not want cats or dogs, smaller mammals, such as mice, gerbils, guinea pigs, or rabbits, can be pleasing alternatives. Most are usually kept in cages to keep them safe from predators, and for reasons of hygiene. For the comfort and health of small animals, their cages must be of a good size. For rabbits or guinea pigs, a large wire cage can be provided for daytime use. This can be put into the yard in good weather and moved around so the animal has access to fresh grass—also a good way of keeping the grass short. Cages must be kept clean, and children should be encouraged to clean them out on a regular basis; soiled straw, hay, and wood shavings can be recycled in the compost heap.

Most species of small mammals will be fairly content in this situation, but birds, which fly free in the wild, become frustrated if kept in cages, and often stop singing or begin to molt. I do not recommend keeping a caged bird, but if you have a large garden with space for a proper aviary, there is no reason not to have birds. Homing pigeons are favored by some people and offer an absorbing pastime. Trained to fly long distances before returning to their pigeon loft, they get plenty of opportunity to exercise their wings.

There are, unfortunately, various downsides to keeping pets, particularly cats and dogs. They require constant attention, which can make vacations difficult, and consume a great deal of food, which is often specially formulated, canned, and packaged for them, adding cost and contributing to the problem of household waste. Cans and foil containers are now recyclable, but plastic may not be. It is often advisable to train cats and dogs to eat scraps and family leftovers, and to give them fresh fish and meat. It is difficult, but not impossible, to convert carnivores to vegetarianism, although most veterinary experts advise that a dog's diet should be one-third meat, mixed with cereals and vegetables; cats need three-quarters of their diet to be composed of meat and/or fish and poultry.

Some vets also specialize in alternative health therapies for pets, using homeopathy, acupuncture, herbs, and even aromatherapy.

FISH

Cats, although beautiful and aesthetically pleasing, are predators, and can kill wild birds, mice, frogs, and even squirrels, which can be distressing for their owners. They may also poach fish from a pond. However, don't scold or punish an animal for bringing in trophies; it is a sign of their natural instincts and of their regard for their owners.

Within the home, animals can do damage. Cats in particular are known to be home wreckers! They will shred upholstery, splinter the legs on furniture, transform the carpet into a fuzzy mess when sharpening their claws, shinny up drapes and curtains, even chew wool blankets, rugs, flooring, and clothes. However, most cats can, and should, be trained to use an alternative, such as a scratching post. All cats should have access to the outside world via a cat flap in either the back or front door.

An untrained dog will also have a tendency to soil sidewalks, which is unhealthy and extremely antisocial, and you need to train your dog to urinate and to excrete feces in the street, next to curb. Always avoid letting your dog foul grassed areas where children play. Dog owners must consider others and when walking their dog should use a plastic bag or "pooper scooper" to scoop up feces, and dispose of it hygienically.

The harmful *Toxocara canis* found in feces can survive in soil for over two years, so your dog should not foul on the lawn or flowerbeds, especially if there are children in the house. Strict hygiene is essential; never eat while playing with an animal. Always wash your hands thoroughly after grooming, feeding, and playing with a pet and teach your children to do the same.

Finally, pets such as cats and dogs should always wear a collar, bearing its name and your address and telephone number. Any dog or cat that will spend time outside the home should also be given a yearly rabies vaccination.

AN AQUARIUM filled with colorful fish can be the ultimate design accessory; it can add color and a constantly moving image to any room in the house. Built into a wall between two rooms, it can create an impression of space, light, and life. But fish are not only beautiful, they are also known to create a soothing environment and have a profoundly calming effect.

Until recently, glass was the only material used for aquariums and fish tanks, but now clear acrylic is available that is safer because it is more shatter-proof. It can also be molded, and aquariums now come in a wide range of shapes, from semiarchitectural structures to the more conventional rectangular fish tank.

Aquariums should be sited where they are both protected and easily visible. Nothing should be placed on top of the tank. You should seek professional advice about which types of fish are most suitable, how many can live in one tank, and which can live together. It is important to avoid overcrowding, which will kill or distress the fish, and to avoid overfeeding.

Aquariums combine water and electricity—to light, pump, aerate, and circulate the water—and if you have any doubts about your ability to install the equipment, consult an expert.

Walking a dog is very enjoyable and a cheap, effective way of keeping fit. Allowing a dog to foul public places, however, is antisocial and spreads disease.

An aquarium full of fish brings beauty and calm into the home.

FISH AND FENG SHUI

Fish in outdoor pools and water features, or inside in aquariums, tanks, or bowls, represent good feng shui because they are believed to bring luck to their owners. They are also known to be soothing and calming, which is why they are recommended for hospital and doctors' and dentists' waiting rooms. In the home, they should be positioned to the east or south-east of the center of your home.

Fish are thought to stimulate chi by their movement, depending on their shape, color, and behavior.

Fast-moving fish, darting back and forth, create a dynamic flow of chi energy; more slow-moving, rounded fish will calm down chi energy. As in interior design, brightly colored fish stimulate the flow of energy; fish of more muted colors will create a more relaxing ambience.

For good feng shui, the tank should be "landscaped" with natural materials such as rocks, shells, and pebbles, combined with appropriate living plants. Plastic decorations must be avoided.

Fish are particularly auspicious in feng shui. Their flowing movements activate healthy chi, and they are believed to stimulate wealth and abundance. But they must be healthy.

There is some evidence that the presence of fish can relieve high blood pressure and lower stress levels. They can make a very positive contribution to a healthy home.

ENCOURAGING WILDLIFE

A wildlife garden is ecologically balanced. Plants attract insects and other creatures that remove pests naturally without pesticides.

ENCOURAGING various species of wild animals into your garden is both life-enhancing and a very natural way of bringing living things into your home. Flowering shrubs, herbs, and scented flowers will all encourage bees and insects, and shrubs such as buddleia, appropriately nicknamed the butterfly bush, will attract one of the most beautiful of wild things—the butterfly, from simple small ones to larger, more exotic varieties. They in turn will pollinate the plants, and bees will make honey from the nectar.

If you have a large enough garden and lots of fruit trees and flowering shrubs and plants, you could consider keeping bees, which is a most rewarding hobby. Site hives well away from the house, and encourage children not to go too close unless accompanied by an adult. They will enjoy helping to harvest the honey and making beeswax candles. My great aunt kept bees in the middle of a cherry orchard, and from a very young age I used to help her; she always insisted that I go and "talk to the bees" on my arrival at her house,

to keep them in touch with what had been happening in my life, and as a result I was never stung.

Wildlife can also help to keep your yard naturally pest-free. Frogs, toads, and water insects in a pond will help to keep the water clean and keep the slug population down; you may also gain the extra benefit of seeing dragonflies hovering over the pond or pool in the summer months.

A healthy garden will also encourage bird life, and their song will be a pleasing addition to your home. If you feed birds, make sure that your feeders are placed in such a way that cats cannot reach the feeding birds. Place bird feeders away from walls, fences, or convenient windowsills and wrap something around the base to prevent cats from climbing up and using it as a dining table. Squirrels, too, are notoriously good at poaching food intended for birds; you can buy feeders that allow birds to eat but are designed to keep other animals at bay.

It is said that if you talk to bees, you won't get stung. Keeping them is a skill, but if you are successful, they will provide you with fresh honey and beeswax.

Because of its delicate color and strong scent, lavender is a popular garden plant that is also grown commercially. Butterflies and bees also find the pungent purple bush irresistible.

CREATING AN ECO-

–FRIENDLY HOME

160
A HEALTHIER HOME

170
A RESOURCE-FRIENDLY HOME

A HOME

In the first section of this book, you have seen how good spatial planning, interesting design, and sensitive use of color and furnishings can all contribute to creating a pleasant ambience and healthy home—where you can live in harmonious surroundings.

But a healthy home is also about safety and environmental friendliness. As home owners, particularly in the West, we consume vast quantities of valuable resources such as water and energy on a relentless day-by-day basis. We also generate mountains of household waste from food to unnecessary packaging. We may also introduce toxic or chemical pollutants into the home in the form of household cleaners, sealants, plastics, and foam-filled furniture, which are themselves unhealthy and contribute to the problems of pollution both inside and outside the home.

Few of us can afford to design and build our own homes from scratch, nor can we necessarily manage to completely redecorate and refurnish every room all at once. Instead, we usually move into a property that will need some initial remedial or cosmetic work before we can turn it into the home we want. It may, for instance, contain some harmful or toxic materials such as lead or asbestos, which are now known to be dangerous.

This section, therefore, looks at some of the toxic substances and other sources of pollution that may already be present in your home and suggests ways of dealing with them. It also offers advice on choosing and using safer, more environmentally friendly products in the home, suggestions on what to keep and what to replace of the existing scheme, and, if you wish, how to apply the ancient principles of feng shui in order to heal your home, correcting a negative or stagnant interior and improving the flow of energy throughout the home.

The following pages also include many practical ways in which you can become more energy- and resource-conscious: by using solar or other forms of renewable energy, by insulating your home to conserve energy, by introducing simple measures to avoid wasting water without losing your quality of life, by cutting down on consumption generally, and by learning to recycle a whole range of household products.

Most of these suggestions can be implemented very easily. Following them not only will mean that your home will be truly healthy and in tune with the environment, but also, in some cases, may provide you with useful and simple ways of saving money.

SURVEYING FOR POLLUTANTS

WHEN WE BUY A NEW HOME, we usually call in an expert to survey it for us and assess its value. The survey will warn of structural faults, subsidence, plumbing and electrical defects, and the need for moisture or infestation control. But we rarely request a survey for pollutants present in the fabric or brought into the home by other means.

Most of us today are aware of the problems and hazards of environmental pollution, but not everyone is aware that the home itself can be polluting. According to the U.S. Environmental Protection Agency, indoor pollution may in some cases be ten times as high as that of the street outside. According to the EPA, air pollution in the home, as well as polluting consumer products, can be serious health risks even though home owners perceive them as less worrying than, say, pollution from landfill sites. Problems can also be intensified by our tendency to overinsulate and seal our homes, thus trapping and circulating unhealthy vapors or gases—one very good reason for remembering to open windows.

Pollutants in the home come in various forms, from invisible radiation to cigarette smoke and dust mites. Other common health hazards include asbestos, lead, pressed boards bound with urea-formaldehyde resins, and plastics. Some, such as asbestos, once commonly used as an insulator, or lead pipes and lead-based paint may already be present in your home, remnants of previously acceptable building practices. Other pollutants, particu-larly various vapors and fumes, may be introduced into the home with the increasing use of chemicals and synthetic materials. Formaldehyde, for instance, is one of the most harmful. Used in literally hundreds of household products and building materials and once commonly used as a cavity wall insulator, it gives off noxious fumes that can cause skin irritation and breathing difficulties. Fortunately, its use is now largely banned. Plastics, too, particularly PVCs (polyvinylchlorides), also produce harmful fumes, as do a whole host of products from cleaning materials to glues, adhesives, and sealants.

Other sources of pollution include radon, an invisible, tasteless, and odorless gas that may be present in the actual structure of the house or seep in from surrounding areas, and other forms of radiation emitted from various household appliances such as computers, televisions, and microwaves.

Not all dangers are obvious—fumes do not always smell—and their effects are usually cumulative. Nor is any one home likely to contain every sort of pollutant. But by and large it is possible to take preventative measures to deal with almost all household pollutants. In the case of existing pollutants, it is best to start by taking professional advice. Asbestos, for instance, must be professionally removed since it becomes truly dangerous only when disturbed. Experts can also advise on the presence of radon, and floors and walls can be sealed or covered with radon-impermeable materials. Installing good ventilation systems, especially in basements and on the ground floor, will also help to clean air. You can minimize pollutants by cutting down on electrical appliances and choosing natural products to clean, decorate, and furnish your home.

Surveying for a new home

If you are buying land on which to build or thinking about a newly built house that is part of a development, check the history of the site. It is not wise to buy or build on top of a landfill site, over a salt, tin, coal, or other mineral mine, over an area with many underground streams, nor near granite, stone, marble, or clay quarry.

If you are building your own home, you may also want to have a geomagnetic survey, which investigates gradients in the earth's magnetic field and establishes the presence of any negative substances that might affect the health of the occupants. The survey is carried out in relation to the contours of the site: distorted trees are regarded as suspicious since they may point to geomagnetic abnormalities, and the surrounding area is measured carefully, usually with a proton magnetometer. The survey should also detect potential areas of radioactivity.

A professional surveyor or architect should plot the results of such a survey on a contoured site plan, so the house can be built in the most favorable position.

Asbestos, once used as insulation around pipes or boilers or in ceiling tiles, must be removed by experts. Removal disturbs asbestos fibers, which can cause respiratory or other disorders

Dust mites can exacerbate asthma

Plastics of all kinds from furniture to packaging release harmful fumes

Cigarette smoke is one of the most serious indoor pollutants. Health risks from active or passive smoking include emphysema, lung cancer, and heart problems

Petrochemical-based paints, stains, or varnishes release harmful fumes

Sulfur dioxide from coal fires

Foam-filled furniture is highly flammable and produces toxic fumes if it combusts

Lead-based paint, once commonly used as a drying agent, is highly poisonous; it must be removed carefully

Nitrogen dioxide or carbon monoxide from badly maintained natural-gas stoves or heaters

Lead pipes can poison water and must be removed

Pesticides and fungicides used in wood treatments can be toxic

Phthalates from vinyl floor tiles and carpet backing

Radon, an invisible gas, that may be present in construction materials or seep in from outside

Houses, whether old or new, may contain a surprising number of pollutants. You should aim to remove them, with professional help if necessary.

Formaldehyde, which is used in cavity-wall insulation, blockboard, disinfectants, carpets, and various building materials, can cause asthma and bronchitis.

Volatile organic compounds in paints, glues, polishes, and construction materials can cause eye irritation, headaches, and possible nerve damage

REMOVING POLLUTANTS

FOR MAXIMUM HEALTH you need to look carefully at the materials used to build, decorate, and furnish your home and change or replace toxic or hazardous substances with natural, nontoxic materials.

WOOD TREATMENTS
You may need professional advice to establish the health of any wood in your home because treatments are not always obvious. Some woods, particularly those on window and door frames, may have been treated with preservative that contains toxic chemicals or creosote. Beams, joists, and roof supports may have been professionally protected against woodworm and rot with substances that are dangerous. If this is the case, you may want to replace certain pieces; others, such as exterior woodwork, could be carefully stripped and a more user-friendly preservative or stain used. Some stains and paints are microporous, allowing wood to breathe, so it is less likely to suffer from damp and decay and will not need restaining or repainting as often.

If you are having wood protected against decay or infestation, or are buying new frames, you can insist on user-friendly materials. Some can be impregnated with a borax that prevents fungus from developing or insect eggs from hatching. This can be injected into existing wood as well, including exterior greenhouses and sheds, and it will not harm plant life.

There are also special natural methods of treating fungal decay. Woodworm and other beetles can be treated with permethrin (a derivative of pyrethrum), or in some cases a special heat treatment, originally developed in Scandinavia, can be used. Always check which materials or chemicals are being used and insist on nontoxic alternatives, even though these are likely to be more expensive and may not carry the same length of guarantee as more conventional treatments.

FLOORINGS
Vinyl floorings are often made to resemble natural products. Commonly used in the home, they are wasteful of natural resources and also release harmful fumes. There are many healthier alternatives available.

Many hard floorings come directly from the earth and are quarried. They include marble, slate, granite, and various natural stones including flagstones. There are also many reconstituted stones now available. Even volcanic lava is now being used for floors. Other natural floorings include quarry and ceramic tiles, terracotta squares, encaustic tiles, and bricks. Many hard floorings will need sealing or treating in some way to make them impervious, but avoid PVC varnishes and sealants in favor of more natural alternatives.

Wood, too, is a natural product that comes in many different forms for flooring, from simple planks, decking, or tongue-and-groove floorboards, to intricately inlaid parquet and special "floating" laminated panels. Most wood needs a nonslip sealant, but here too environmentally friendly substances are available. If you are installing a new wood floor, consider using recycled lumber.

Some resilient floorings are also made from natural materials. Cork, for example, comes from the bark of the cork oak tree and is then made into tiles. These need sealing so they do not swell and "push up" if they get wet, and they must be laid on a damp-proofed subfloor. There are some presealed tiles available, which are best for "wet" situations. Cork is not only ecologically sound but is also a very good insulator, and it is warm and comfortable underfoot.

Linoleum is obtained from natural materials: linseed oil, resin from pine trees, wood flour from deciduous trees mixed with inorganic fillers, such as chalk, and pressed onto a burlap or jute backing, then cured in special drying ovens, creating a very flexible, durable, and resilient floor. Linoleum can be bought in sheet form or as tiles.

Rubber is another natural product. Made from the liquid sap of the rubber tree, it is available as tiles and in sheet form, often has an interestingly textured surface, and comes in some stunning colors. It is bouncy and quiet underfoot, but needs sealing with a special sealant because it deteriorates if it becomes too wet.

There are softer options—the so-called natural floorings such as sisal and seagrass matting, coir (coconut) matting, rush matting, jute, and hemp. These are mostly available in their natural or neutral colors, although they can be dyed, stenciled with a pattern, or trimmed with a decorative border. Many of them have a backing for extra stability, but make sure that it is natural rubber rather than vinyl.

Carpets have long been the popular choice for underfoot luxury, but do choose a natural fiber: 100 percent wool, an 80/20 blend (80 percent wool/20 percent nylon), or cotton. Some more exotic carpets and rugs are made from silk. Some carpets and other soft floor coverings have been treated with chemicals to make them stain- and dirt-repellent and to bulk up pile, and all these treatments are toxic,

so check floor coverings before buying. It is possible to remove the chemicals with cleaning, but it would be better to avoid them altogether.

FABRICS AND SOFT FURNISHINGS

Always try to use natural rather than artificial fibers in the home. For upholstery consider wool, cotton, linen, silk, or their various combinations. One durable fabric used for slipcovers and some upholstery is a blend of linen and cotton. Some blends, however, contain a small quantity of artificial fibers, which will make them crease-resistant and easier to launder. You will have to weigh the advantages of ease of care against the disadvantages of not using a totally natural product.

Buying natural fibers is not always as ecologically sound as we might think. Many cotton and linen growers use pesticides, although there are organic cotton growers who use integrated pest management to control insects. Cotton is usually bleached after harvesting and then dyed, and

linen may be similarly treated, although it is far better to buy linen that has been bleached in natural sunlight. It is also possible to buy bed linens, bath towels, and some curtain and slipcover fabrics that are unbleached, undyed, and untreated, so ask the supplier or manufacturer for the "history" of the fabric. Unfortunately, organically produced cotton and untreated natural fibers are likely to be more expensive.

WALL COVERINGS

Wallpaper is readily available and far more appropriate than a vinyl wall covering, which is actually printed onto a PVC sheet and then backed with paper, making an impervious wall surface that prevents the wall underneath from breathing. Plastic wall coverings made from foamed polyethylene should be avoided. As yet I have not heard of a wall covering made from recycled paper, but I am sure this will come soon. Meanwhile, natural brown and green wrapping paper, newspapers, even gift wrap and book endpapers can be used to decorate walls successfully. Or you might prefer to use paint on your walls, which can of course be put on over wood chip paper.

PAINTS, STAINS, AND FINISHES

Paint is probably one of the most useful materials for healing your home cosmetically. You can use it on walls, ceilings, floors, woodwork, and metalwork. Highly versatile, paint comes in almost every color you can think of. But you must use the right paint for the job. Some paints are only suitable for walls or ceilings; others are more appropriate for wood or metal.

Stains and varnishes are usually applied to wood furniture, to enhance the finish, bringing up the natural grain of the wood, or to produce a decorative treatment.

Check the contents of paints, primers, and varnishes very carefully. Most paints once contained lead, now known to be poisonous, as a drying agent, It is being phased out, but check to make sure your paint is leadfree. Older paint layers around your home may contain lead, so remove and replace them very carefully.

Some paints and varnishes, particularly gloss finishes, may also contain solvents or other harmful chemicals, and most are petrochemically based. A natural resin such as shellac, used as a varnish and to prevent knots in wood from showing through the top surface, is infinitely preferable to one containing polyurethane and can be used to seal bonded and other chemically treated building materials such as particleboard, blockboard, or plywood.

There are other natural resin-based varnishes. Some organic paint manufacturers make a microporous varnish which is user-friendly, does not emit fumes, and is biodegradable. For exterior use, it has to be tinted with pigment to protect wood from ultraviolet rays, but inside it can be used in its natural form.

There are organic oil-based paints, which can be used on wood, stone, and metal, indoors and out. These are based on plant oils, resins, and other natural ingredients. Color is provided by adding pure earth pigments. Organic masonry paints are available for exterior stonework and stucco. Alternatively you can use traditional limewash, tinted with natural pigments.

Most water-based paints such as distemper or latex are less likely to contain harmful ingredients but are only suitable for walls and ceilings. They can be applied directly onto plaster, plasterboard, or paper. Paint manufacturers are currently experimenting with water-based gloss paints that can be used on woodwork and metal. There are organic wall latex paints, which usually come in white or a very limited choice of colors, but you can color them to your own recipe with natural pigments. Trad-itional distemper and milk (casein) paints are also made from natural ingredients; again, you can add the color yourself.

Finally, if you have the time, you could make your own paints, which will give you the chance to create unique colors and finishes; recipes are available from local stores. Water-based paints are easier to make: distemper or lime-wash is mixed in a bucket with water, pigment is added, and you are ready to go!

FURNITURE

Synthetic sealants or spray polishes for wooden furniture and surfaces frequently contain harmful chemicals; as aerosols, too, they make use of CFCs that damage the ozone layer. Avoid them. You can either use nonpolluting alternatives or traditional products such as beeswax or natural oils. These are more eco-friendly and smell good. Linseed oil is often used to treat bare wood, but it can yellow the surface. Again, you can make your own furniture polish: turpentine mixed with linseed oil; olive oil with vinegar; or vegetable oil with lemon juice.

Use one of the organic paints or eco-friendly stains or sealants to paint furniture. If you are stripping off a previous surface, avoid caustic strippers, which can be highly toxic and also damaging. Sanding wood is preferable, but wear a face mask for safety while sanding.

Use natural fabrics or leather to upholster furniture. Avoid vinyl or PVC, which can cause various disorders. The ubiquitous plastic foam, which became popular some twenty years ago, is now known to be a serious fire hazard. Fumes given off from the smoldering foam are highly toxic and can be fatal. Do not buy any furniture which contains this foam and remove any already in your house. Instead, use natural products for fillings such as flock (made from cotton waste), horsehair, wool, pure down, or a feather and down mixture. If somebody in your household is allergic to any of these, he or she could use a foam-rubber-filled mattress, but make sure there is a special barrier fabric, covering the foam and under the top cover, as a fire retardant. Pillows, quilts, and comforters can be filled with cotton (like the mattresses on futons), foam rubber, or wool.

Today, new domestic upholstery has to pass a cigarette and match test for safety. Some natural fabrics, such as wool, may be inherently flame-retardant; fabrics can also be treated, but fire-retarding products contain potentially toxic chemicals.

Encouraging sustainability

Most new kitchens, bathrooms, and built-in bedrooms are made from what is known as composite board or laminated board, neither of which are particularly environmentally friendly. Natural wood is obviously healthier, but if you are worried about threats to rain or other forests, you can stipulate wood from quick-growing sustainable sources. Some environmentally aware kitchen and other furniture specialists even promise to plant a tree for every kitchen or bedroom they install, so helping to replenish natural resources. If you are concerned about the overuse of natural materials, ask suppliers about their policy on "plundering the planet" and follow your conscience. Friends of the Earth and other conservation and environmental groups will give advice and recommend manufacturers and stockists.

Using natural wood in your home is certainly healthier, but does pose an environmental dilemma; if you are at all worried, look for manufacturers who pledge to replenish the trees that they use.

HOME
SAFE
HOME

THE HEALTHY HOME should be a safe home. Every year literally thousands of people suffer accidents, some fatal, because their homes are poorly organized or designed. Common accidents include scalding or burning from unguarded fires or cooking utensils; falls or trips because of awkwardly placed furniture, poor lighting, or badly-fitting carpets; cuts or other injuries from sharp implements or rough surfaces; and general bumping and bruising. Poisoning and electrical accidents are also common.

However, most accidents in the home can be avoided by taking simple precautions.

All toxic or poisonous substances from disinfectants through to decorating materials and medicines should be kept safely locked away. Cutting implements from knives to gardening tools should always be stored safely.

In the kitchen, potentially one of the most dangerous rooms in the house, make sure that hot pans are guarded and cannot be pulled over. To avoid the risk of fire, keep a fire blanket close to the stove and invest in fire extinguishers that can be strategically placed throughout the house in case of need.

Tall houses need an outside fire escape. If you live in an apartment building, check the fire exits and make sure fire doors are always accessible and free from clutter. You can also buy special rope ladders, which can be thrown down from upper windows in case of an emergency. Think about the risk of fire and work out a suitable drill. Keep corridors and doors free of clutter for easy access into and out of rooms.

Glass and glazing are a feature of most houses. However, make sure that all windows can be opened easily in case of an emergency.

Good lighting is essential. A house that is well lit during the day and night should be accident-free. Make sure that corners, the insides of deep cupboards, stair treads, and changes of level, inside and outdoors, are well lighted. Also light front and back doors, house names, and house numbers.

Keep electrical equipment well maintained and switched off when not in use. Use circuit breakers outdoors and lock away specialized or expensive equipment. If you use candles or kinetic lighting, make sure they are extinguished when you leave the room.

Make sure that all floors are nonslip. If you use rugs, make sure they are secure and not liable to slipping or creeping. Check and maintain all carpets to make sure they are in good condition. Deal immediately with any holes or ravels. Stair carpets are particularly vulnerable.

Furniture and fixtures should stand firm, level, and square, and not be in danger of toppling over.

Cribs, playpens, and other children's furniture should be designed for safety and free from toxic paints. Use nonflammable and natural materials for sofas, chairs, and other furniture.

Water features should be planned with care, particularly if there are young children around.

Security is an important aspect of safety. Consult a specialist for advice and use a professional to install locks, window bolts, and other security devices according to your personal needs.

Finally, keep a comprehensive first-aid kit conveniently on hand. Keep a list of emergency numbers by the telephone.

Do-It-Yourself Safety
Think health and safety when doing any D.I.Y. Work in dry, well-ventilated areas and protect yourself if using toxic materials. Keep tools well maintained and wear a face mask and goggles if sanding floors or cutting glass or ceramics. Work at a bench, using a vice to grip items. Keep paints, stains, and varnishes well sealed.

You can introduce some simple precautions to make your home a safer place.

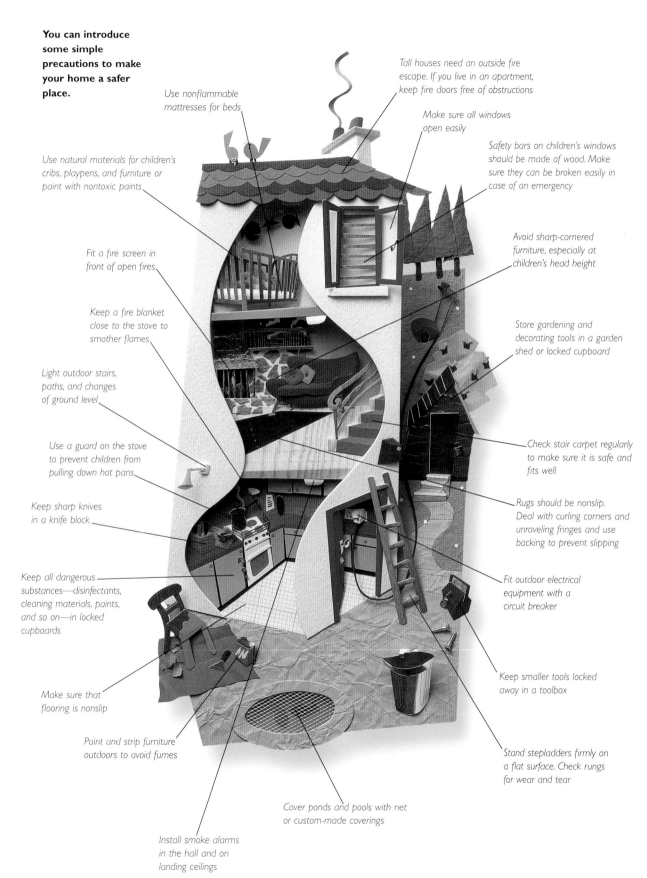

Use nonflammable mattresses for beds

Tall houses need an outside fire escape. If you live in an apartment, keep fire doors free of obstructions

Make sure all windows open easily

Safety bars on children's windows should be made of wood. Make sure they can be broken easily in case of an emergency

Use natural materials for children's cribs, playpens, and furniture or paint with nontoxic paints

Avoid sharp-cornered furniture, especially at children's head height

Fit a fire screen in front of open fires

Keep a fire blanket close to the stove to smother flames

Store gardening and decorating tools in a garden shed or locked cupboard

Light outdoor stairs, paths, and changes of ground level

Use a guard on the stove to prevent children from pulling down hot pans

Check stair carpet regularly to make sure it is safe and fits well

Rugs should be nonslip. Deal with curling corners and unraveling fringes and use backing to prevent slipping

Keep sharp knives in a knife block

Keep all dangerous substances—disinfectants, cleaning materials, paints, and so on—in locked cupboards

Fit outdoor electrical equipment with a circuit breaker

Keep smaller tools locked away in a toolbox

Make sure that flooring is nonslip

Paint and strip furniture outdoors to avoid fumes

Stand stepladders firmly on a flat surface. Check rungs for wear and tear

Cover ponds and pools with net or custom-made coverings

Install smoke alarms in the hall and on landing ceilings

HEALING WITH FENG SHUI

Feng shui can be used in many ways to enhance the health of your home and your general wellbeing. At the outset you can use the principles of feng shui to plan the purpose, layout, and contents of your rooms in the most favorable ways. But you can also use feng shui to "cure" existing faults that may be causing energy problems. Most cures involve the use of healthy plants, mirrors, and light, and offer simple and inexpensive ways of increasing favorable chi in the home. You can do them yourself or, if problems are severe, ask a feng shui consultant for advice.

Growing plants both indoors and out can do much to improve energy flows. Placed on the front doorstep or on each side of a path, they provide welcome and prevent energy from flowing out of the home. Staggered plants in the hall also slow down fast-moving chi. Placed in the kitchen or the work room, plants also help to counteract radiation emissions. Spiky plants, too, such as yuccas, can prevent stagnant chi from gathering in a corner.

Corners thrusting into a room or angular-shaped furniture are said to create harmful cutting chi, known as "poison arrows." This can be softened and deflected by standing a large plant in front of the offending corner, or by trailing a plant over it. L-shaped rooms, too, cause energy imbalance and can be corrected by placing a mirror on one of the walls on the inside of the "L" to increase a sense of space.

Neighboring buildings can also cause cutting chi if a sharp corner points toward your home. Planting bushes or trees near the front door, or placing reflective surfaces near the front door to deflect the chi, will solve the problem.

Exposed structural beams are also likely to cause cutting or negative chi, especially if they are made of steel or concrete. In a high-ceilinged room, the negative effects are weakened, but using uplighters or tall leafy plants will further reduce the effect.

Internal corners can cause stagnant chi, so speed up the energy by reflecting light from glossy-leaved plants, shiny textures, or mirrors. Good lighting and pleasant sounds will also keep energy flowing.

Warnings:

Never position mirrors opposite each other as energy will bounce from one to the other.

Do not put mirrors opposite a door or window as this will reflect back energy entering the room.

Avoid mirrors or mirror tiles that distort the body.

Light and freedom from clutter are both integral to the feng shui philosophy. Too much clutter can cause stagnation, so organize your possessions well, put things away neatly, and do a major clearing and reorganization occasionally. Make sure potentially dark areas are well lighted.

MIRRORS Mirrors often provide simple solutions. They redirect the flow of energy and light waves, intensifying light and creating an impression of greater space. Shiny metal, reflective glass, highly polished furniture, and glazed ceramic tiles can all have similar effects.

Circular mirrors reflect chi energy in several directions, spreading it out and helping to disperse fast-moving or cutting chi. Flat mirrors reflect in just one direction. Octagonal mirrors are particularly significant, their eight sides reflecting the eight directions of the compass. Low, wide, rectangular mirrors create a stable, calm atmosphere; tall, thin rectangular mirrors encourage upward-moving energy.

Careful positioning of mirrors helps to move chi harmoniously through the home. If you have a long, narrow corridor or hall, slow energy down by positioning staggered mirrors on opposite walls. If stairs face the front door, there is a danger that chi will flow out of the house and disappear; place a large, flat mirror next to the front door to reflect energy back into the house. To be most effective, mirrors should be sparkling clean.

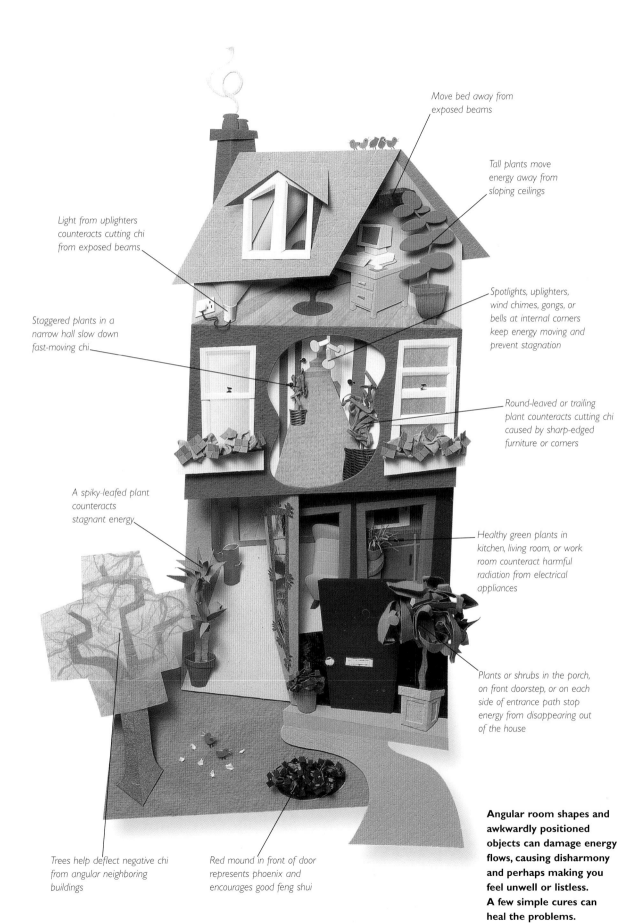

Move bed away from
exposed beams

Tall plants move
energy away from
sloping ceilings

Light from uplighters
counteracts cutting chi
from exposed beams

Spotlights, uplighters,
wind chimes, gongs, or
bells at internal corners
keep energy moving and
prevent stagnation

Staggered plants in a
narrow hall slow down
fast-moving chi

Round-leaved or trailing
plant counteracts cutting chi
caused by sharp-edged
furniture or corners

A spiky-leafed plant
counteracts
stagnant energy

Healthy green plants in
kitchen, living room, or work
room counteract harmful
radiation from electrical
appliances

Plants or shrubs in the porch,
on front doorstep, or on each
side of entrance path stop
energy from disappearing out
of the house

Trees help deflect negative chi
from angular neighboring
buildings

Red mound in front of door
represents phoenix and
encourages good feng shui

**Angular room shapes and
awkwardly positioned
objects can damage energy
flows, causing disharmony
and perhaps making you
feel unwell or listless.
A few simple cures can
heal the problems.**

SECOND TIME AROUND

WE HAVE AT LAST WAKED up to the dreadful vandalism perpetrated on buildings and houses in the name of progress during the first sixty years of the 20th century. Today the trend is toward preserving our heritage, protecting or restoring buildings and architectural features, in some cases completely restoring a property to its original architectural style and glory. Conversions, too, such as factories and warehouse remodeling into living spaces, are now done in a more sympathetic way, with great consideration for the overall look and its place in the local environment.

Fortunately many traditional building materials and architectural items, such as windows, doors, plasterwork, fireplaces, stoves, cornices, moldings, and paneling, have been saved and are still available for reuse. There are also many builder's yards that specialize in salvaged and recycled products. Increasingly, too, there is an army of people who are training in traditional crafts and can help with restoration of wood, plaster, stone, and even thatching. Some are involved in prestigious projects, restoring historic buildings such as London's Westminster Abbey; others are available to help designers, architects, and home owners on less complex projects.

However, before you rush to call in an expert, it is worthwhile looking carefully at your home to see how much of the original structure still exists, perhaps hidden away behind wallboard, tiling, or wall-to-wall carpets. Floors made from terracotta squares, flagstones, slate, inlaid parquet, quarry, or encaustic tiles may be hiding under a layer or two of linoleum, vinyl, or underfelt and carpet. If you don't want this type of flooring, or any other original feature you may discover hidden away, don't destroy it; have it taken up, or out, very carefully by a salvage expert so it can be reused in a different area of your home, or by somebody else. Your

One of the starting points for an eco-friendly home is to reuse or restore wherever possible. Before you rush out to buy, take a careful look at your own home. You may find that behind an old piece of board is a beautiful fireplace.

Always check old wood for woodworm before reusing it and bringing it into your home.

"white elephant" may be someone else's source of enjoyment, and may bring you some extra cash.

On the other hand, if you do want interesting architectural features or a traditional floor, you should be able to find suitable materials and old floorings and have them relaid in your home. Look out for rich terracotta tiles, golden flagstones, and subtle slates that have been reclaimed from old houses. These tend to have a wonderfully warm quality and a patina of age that makes them a joy to live with.

If you want wooden floors, you may be able to restore, repair, strip, sand, and seal existing floorboards. If they are very worn, painted, or heavily stained, you can take them up, turn them over, and relay them, effectively creating new boards that will have the advantage of being cut to size and shape as well as being well seasoned.

Such restoration is practical only if you are planning a fair bit of rebuilding because it will involve structural work such as removing baseboards and repairing joists. However, once you have your new surface, you can decorate it to taste: stenciling, marbling, or even handpainting.

SALVAGING AND RECYCLING

Reusing salvaged items may not necessarily mean restoring the things found in your own home. Enterprising designers, furniture specialists, carpenters, and manufacturing companies are making new furniture, accessories, sculptures, and

An increasing number of designers and furniture makers are producing furniture and fittings made from recycled furniture, which you can buy. If appropriate, you can also strip surfaces back to reveal original brickwork and beams.

other decorative objects from recycled materials such as old beams and paneling, driftwood, or old railroad ties, all of which can take a new lease on life converted into tables, benches, and cupboards. Old, heavy, and unattractive pieces of furniture, to our eyes, can also be dismantled (originally many of them were built to come apart easily) and re-shaped as several smaller items.

I once bought an enormous Victorian mahogany and satinwood armoire, sitting on a base of two large drawers, with two storage cupboards on each side, and a set of drawers and small chests in the center, all joined by a heavy carved cornice on top. I took it apart, used the base to make a bench and toy chest and the cornice to make a decorative window valence, placed

the cupboards, now freestanding, in the kitchen, and put the drawers and small chests in my study, for extra storage.

Some designers specialize in trawling dumpsters and local dumping sites, converting well-seasoned lumber, malleable metal, or other pliant materials into useful household items or eye-catching art forms. There is no reason why you should not join this band of creative magpies, although it is, of course, only good manners to ask the household or builder if you can take something out of their dumpster.

Other hunting grounds for recyclable materials include forests or woodlands, where branches and trees may have fallen in a storm, seashores, canals, and river banks. Driftwood can be converted into doors, tables, chairs, kitchen furniture, and so on, or crafted into models and sculptures. It can also be a decorative accessory in its own right, particularly when combined with indoor plants. Larger pieces, which may have been left stranded by the tide or discovered half-buried in mud, can be used for furniture. Many rustic garden benches, for instance, began life as something different.

Recycling need not be confined to the re-use of wood and metal. Small scraps of fabric can be recycled for herb pillows, or stitched into patchwork for quilts and pillows or pegged or plaited into rag rugs. Antique textiles, too, such as pieces of tapestry, embroidery, old lace, or velvet, can be converted into cushions, table covers, lamp shades, and other accessories.

Many textiles and rugs can be used as decorative wall hangings, and I have seen some damaged kilim rugs cut down and used for upholstery for stools, small chairs, and floor cushions. There are experts who specialize in this sort of work, but these are crafts that you can learn to do yourself. Furniture, too, can be given a new lease on life by mending or reupholstering, and again, this is a craft you can learn.

Many household items, from glass bottles and jars to plastic containers, can also be recycled for use in your own home, perhaps as storage jars or plant or candle holders. Paper can be recycled creatively within your house rather than being taken to a recycling center. Papier-mâché, made from torn or shredded paper bound with flour-and-water paste, is very easy to make and can be used for a variety of objects. In the late 19th

The number of businesses dealing in salvaged materials from old properties has increased in the past few years. They provide a happy hunting ground for beautiful old tiles and even larger items such as a kitchen range.

Reduce, reuse, and recycle are the three Rs of resource consciousness. Much household waste—paper, cans, glass, food—can be recycled. But recycling is not an end in itself. We should also reduce consumption and reuse whatever we can.

century, papier-mâché was used for making furniture, trays, bowls, decorative plates, and paintings. In some cases, the objects were inlaid with mother of pearl. It has even been used for buildings; a Norwegian church, for instance, was built from paper that was recycled in this way.

Old ceramic tiles can be recycled to create a patchwork wall or floor, using flooring-grade tiles. Alternatively, broken pieces can be used to make decorative mosaics in bathrooms and kitchens or to convert ordinary flowerpots, windowboxes, and tubs into more decorative containers.

Glass, too, can be recycled for decorative use, perhaps cut and leaded into stained-glass panels. Broken car windshield glass, which has dull edges, has also been recycled creatively. Combined with gravel, it can give added glitter to a path or patio.

RECYCLING WASTE

It has been estimated that at least 80 percent of all our household waste could be recycled. This includes paper, glass, food waste, and clothing. And these days most towns and cities provide a variety of recycling facilities.

Appropriately enough, my city provides green containers for unwanted glass bottles, jars, cans, paper, and fabrics, which then are taken away weekly.

But as well as recycling and reusing, you should also aim to reduce consumption in order to avoid generating yet more waste. Try not to buy too much prepackaged food and other products. Reuse plastic shopping bags or ask for paper bags, which can be recycled, in preference to plastic and other nonbiodegradable packaging. Buy drinks, milk, cosmetics, and other products in glass containers rather than plastic. Invest in a water purifier and seltzer maker so you can make your own drinks. Try making your own wine, jams, chutneys, and preserves as well, remembering to recycle the containers each time.

Recycle all kitchen or food waste. If you live in a rural area, you may be able to give some to a nearby farm for animal food, or even keep and feed your own livestock such as ducks, geese, or chickens. If this is not possible, turn your food scraps into compost for use in your garden.

Sort household waste carefully; separating the various types of waste is crucial to any successful recycling program. Separate and store waste in one place, ideally close to the kitchen or in a utility area or garage where it will remain dry. Use separate bins for different kinds of waste, perhaps color coded for recognition. They should be handy for pickup and transport to a recycling site. Rinse glass bottles, jars, and cans. If you are recycling aluminum foil containers, rinse them before taking them to the recycling center. Hazardous waste such as old batteries, plastics, paint, paint thinners, and other caustic liquids should be sealed and disposed of safely, perhaps in a landfill.

Large metal and aluminum items, old household appliances, and furniture can also be recycled and reused. You could give them directly to a charity or arrange for pickup by the relevant organization or specialized collector. Check the list of Useful Addresses on page 184, under Recycling, for sources that can offer advice.

A RESOURCE-FRIENDLY HOME

HEALTHY HOUSEKEEPING

A HEALTHY HOME should be clean and free of clutter. But an exhausted housekeeper and children being continually nagged not to make a mess is not conducive to healthy living. An overclean home can be very sterile, so aim for a healthy compromise between hygiene and comfort.

In addition to using healthy materials to decorate and furnish your home, you should use friendly and healthy products to clean it. Many eco-friendly cleaning products are available today, but you can also use various environmentally friendly methods used by our grandmothers and great-grandmothers.

CLEANING AND WASHING MATERIALS
Many of these are environmental hazards. Washing powders and liquids contain bleaching agents or detergents that can irritate the skin, possibly causing allergic reactions. Long-term, they can also destroy fibers in textiles, causing fabrics to rot, wear out, and lose color. When these cleaners are flushed away, the water-polluting phosphates take a long time to break down, causing problems to both fish and plant life.

The alternative is to use some of the now widely available phosphate-free biodegradable products. These include liquid detergent, fabric conditioners, and clothes washing liquids, powders, and conditioners. Containing natural oils and plant extracts, they are nonpolluting and nonirritating.

You can also freshen and soften your clothes by adding 1 teaspoonful of white vinegar or bicarbonate of soda to the final rinse. And there is no better way of achieving fresh-smelling linens and clothes than by hanging them out to dry naturally in the air and sunshine—and you will save energy. For washing dishes, you can use plain, pure soap, adding a little lemon juice or white vinegar if there is grease to contend with.

BLEACHES AND SCOURING POWDERS
or other "dirt-busting" liquids are also hazardous—have you noticed how advertisements frequently suggest an army of strong men is helping to rid your home of dirt with the muscle power contained in their particular product? These products contain chlorine compounds, which give off toxic fumes that irritate both skin and surfaces. Bleach burns the skin, is highly toxic if swallowed, and damages fabric. Some scouring powders and cleansers contain ammonia. If chlorine-containing cleansers are mixed

Bleaches and detergents damage the skin and cause long-term harm to the environment. You can replace them with ready-made eco-friendly products or make your own cleaners using vinegar, horsetail, and bicarbonate of soda.

Vinegar

Horsetail

Bicarbonate of soda

Bleaches

Corrosive cleaners

Salt

Soda

Foil

Silverware

Most metal cleaners are corrosive. You can clean silverware with an environmentally friendly mixture of salt, water, soda, and silver foil.

with ammonia-containing substances, they will give off chloramine gas, which is poisonous.

General-purpose biodegradable cleaners are available, but you can also make your own healthy cleaners with bicarbonate of soda. Mix it into a paste and leave on a dirty surface for a few minutes before rinsing off or use it undiluted on a damp sponge. Fine wood ash and horsetail (a wild plant) is also a good natural scourer. And you can pour white vinegar into the toilet bowl and leave it overnight to freshen, cleanse, and whiten. Use a mild borax or tea tree essential oil *(Melaleuca alternifolia)* solution to disinfect.

FLOOR, FURNITURE, AND METAL POLISHES

can also give off fumes or cause skin irritation. In their aerosol form, they discharge particles of chemical solvents into the air, to say nothing of being ozone-damaging if the propellant contains CFCs. Metal polishes can also be highly corrosive and poisonous. Spray-on polish leaves a deposit on the surface of furniture, which eventually causes it to cloud, and it may then have to be stripped and refinished.

Instead of these, use natural furniture polishes, such as beeswax, mixtures of oil and lemon, or vinegar, which will give your furniture a rich patina. Carnuba wax

can be used for floors, or they can be sealed with a button polish made from a natural resin. Buff occasionally with a mop, but don't make the surface too wet. Wooden floors need "feeding," but other floors, such as linoleum or sealed cork, do not; an occasional mop with soapy water, rinsed with fresh water, will be enough.

You can also make your own cleaner for metals such as silver. Put a sheet of aluminum foil or some old foil tops and containers into a pan, cover with about 2 to 3 inches of water, add 1 teaspoonful salt and 1 teaspoonful bicarbonate of soda, or 1 tablespoon of washing powder, such as borax, and bring to a boil. Drop in small items of silverware and boil for about 3 minutes. Remove them and rinse, then buff with chamois leather or a soft cloth. To clean very small items, or delicate items of jewelry, you can use toothpaste or rubbing alcohol applied with a paintbrush or toothbrush. You can make a pot of dip-in cleaner for small items of jewelry or fork tines by shredding foil to half-fill a screw-top jar. Add a tablespoon of

A cut lemon dipped in salt cleans most kitchen surfaces; boiling gooseberries scours the pan, and vinegar cleans toilets and baths.

salt, fill with water and shake, Put small items in for about 2 to 3 minutes, then rinse, dry, and buff with a cloth.

NATURAL GENERAL CLEANERS

There are many ways of cleaning with natural products such as bicarbonate of soda or lemons, all of them more user-friendly than spray-on caustic solutions. A lemon cut in half and dipped in salt will clean copper, brass, work surfaces, chopping boards, or the inside of a microwave oven. Vinegar will remove mineral deposits from the tub and toilet, and can be used to clean mirrors and windows (buff them afterward with a pad of old newspaper) and to bleach marble surfaces. Stains can be removed from metal saucepans by rubbing with cream of tartar or by cooking rhubarb in them.

Vinegar

Lemon

Gooseberries

Cream of tartar

CONSERVING ENERGY

WE ARE NOW WELL AWARE of the urgent need to conserve resources such as energy and water. On a day-to-day basis this can be done in quite simple ways, such as switching off lights when they are not needed, using energy-saving or low-voltage bulbs, or turning the heating thermostat down a notch or two. Measures such as these not only reduce energy consumption, they will also reduce your bills by as much as 40 to 60 percent.

Other energy-conservation measures, such as roof or floor insulation, insulating hot-water tanks, or installing double glazing, may be more complex to implement and will involve an initial financial outlay. But they do help conserve valuable resources and will eventually pay for themselves.

Fossil fuels such as coal and oil are being rapidly depleted; other sources of energy such as nuclear-generated electricity carry their own environmental risks. Most of us, however, use electricity or gas for home needs, so to minimize consumption, we need to consider the most efficient ways of using them.

As a general rule, electricity is most efficient for high-grade energy needs such as light and powering home and work appliances; while gas, oil, and solid fuels such as coal, anthracite, or coke are best kept for space and water heating.

CHOOSING AND USING APPLIANCES
Choose a really well-designed system that will provide heat for cooking, heating, and water. You can base this on an energy-efficient stove, which will heat water and act as a range. Alternatively, use a wood-, gas-, or coal-fired stove, possibly in a central fireplace, combined with a boiler that will heat water and supply warmth to a few radiators. The stove doors can be opened to provide further radiant heat. Installation may be costly and involve structural work, but is worth considering if you are moving into a new home or making major alterations to your existing home. If you are redesigning your kitchen, for instance, get rid of the conventional heater and stove and replace them with a range that will perform various functions, including drying clothes.

When buying new household appliances such as a washing machine or dishwasher, choose those with energy-saving features such as economy cycles. Remember to use these appliances only when they are full; by doing so, you will actually use less water and heat than when washing by hand. You can also save energy by switching off a dishwasher once it reaches the drying cycle, opening the door, pulling out the shelves, and letting the dishes dry in the warm air. Try to choose appliances that can be filled from your hot-water supply rather than appliances that have their own heaters.

To save energy, dry clothes in the open air whenever possible, perhaps using the spin cycle or a spin dryer to remove excess moisture or use drying racks that can be placed near radiators or sources of radiant heat.

It is up to you to decide how many appliances you really need. Think carefully before buying and using too many electrical

Drying clothes in the open air avoids using electricity.

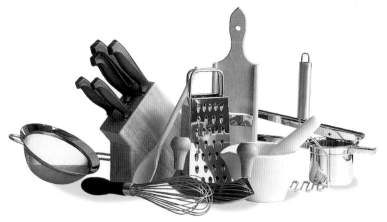

Hand-held kitchen equipment—sharp knives, grater, whisk, strainer, pestle and mortar—can replace electrical appliances.

appliances, and perhaps reassess how often you really need to use them. Do you really need to use a vacuum cleaner every day? A simple damp or dry mopping or a onceover with a carpet sweeper is a good energy-saving compromise. Let your hair dry naturally rather than using a hairdryer. If appropriate, use a kettle to heat water for tea and coffee. Look at kitchen appliances critically. Most kitchens have electrical gadgets tucked away in a corner, gathering dust and never used. Reassess the situation; only keep what you actually use. Used creatively, balloon whisks, wooden spoons, sharp cooking knives, graters, mandolin slicers, and hand-operated vegetable ricers can chop and blend food as efficiently as most electric mixers.

Save energy when you are cooking. Fill the kettle only with the amount of water you need. Don't use the broiler for a single piece of toast. Develop the art of slow cooking with electric slow cookers, which use very little energy. Cook several items from one energy source. For instance, use a tiered steam basket to steam several items at the same time. Put lids on saucepans and turn the heat down once the contents have boiled. Use a heat diffuser to spread the flame for slow simmering; turn off electric stoves before the food is completely cooked—the remaining heat will complete

the process. A convection oven using a fan will use less energy than a conventional oven, as cooking times will be shorter and temperatures slightly lower. Pressure cookers can be used to cook several items of food at once. And if you are cooking small quantities, use a microwave.

Use your oven efficiently, too. Try to cook several dishes at the same time; you might be cooking a main dish and vegetables, but also cook some fruit (fresh or dried) or beans, baked potatoes, or a pudding. If you are buying a new stove, consider one that has two ovens—a smaller one for everyday use and fewer dishes, and a larger one for family and celebratory meals. A griddle pan is often an economical and healthy way of cooking food.

At the other end of the heat scale, use your refrigerator economically. Is it really necessary to have a top-of-the-line self-defrosting monster in the corner? If you have a cool-storage place for food, it is often much better to keep all but the most perishable items there. In some locations, a food cupboard or "meat safe" can be placed in a cool, shady place outside, against a north-facing wall, with a well-ventilated wire grille instead of doors.

If you are buying a new fridge or freezer, the chest type is more economical than the pull-out drawer type. Check for energy

efficiency and make sure it has a non-CFC coolant. Defrost refrigerators regularly for efficiency, and ideally position freezers or refrigerators on an outside, preferably north, wall away from the boiler or stove. Site a freezer in a utility room, shed, or garage. Freezers work more efficiently if they are full. This does not mean you have to rush out to buy frozen items or prepare fresh food for freezing; you can fill spaces with loaves of bread or even clean towels.

Service all appliances regularly so they operate as efficiently as possible. Keep larger items such as washing machines, boilers, and heaters well ventilated and clear of dust, animal hairs, and food; a clogged system may have to work twice as hard, thus using greater amounts of energy.

To save energy, consider using a multi-layered steamer, often also seen in bamboo, to cook three courses or dishes at the same time.

INSULATION Adequate insulation also helps to conserve energy by minimizing heat loss. The amount of work you need to do will very much depend on your particular home: an apartment, row house, or duplex is always warmer than a separate building because of the walls in common with the neighboring property. You also need to consider climate, prevailing winds, shade, and the orientation of your home.

Methods of insulation include wrapping water pipes and storage tanks, insulating an attic, putting a jacket on a hot-water tank, and insulating exterior walls either with cavity insulation or external or internal insulation to solid walls. You can also reduce heat loss by insulating the basement, insulating ground floors, and double-glazing windows to reduce heat loss. You can do many simple insulation jobs yourself—wrapping pipes, installing draft prevention devices—but others are more complex and you will need the assistance of a professional.

Building a porch onto a front or back door or adding a sunroom also cuts down on drafts and traps sunlight, creating a solar-energy-type light and heat source.

If you have conventional central heating, the positioning of radiators is important. It is more efficient to place radiators against an internal wall, rather than under a window, allowing heat to disappear outside. Windows and their frames should be draftproof, to prevent cold air from entering. Place reflective foil on the wall behind the radiator to reflect heat and, if you wish, place a shelf or sill above the radiator to deflect hot air. Radiator covers can be elegant, but they cut the flow of warm air. It is better to disguise a radiator by painting it to blend in with its background. Install thermostats to conserve energy.

Doing your own draft-proofing is a good, cheap, and easy way to insulate some parts of your home. Put draft strips on badly fitting

Lighting efficiency tips

- Switch lights off when you are not using them
- Use a dimmer switch to control light and reduce use of power
- Use low-wattage bulbs where small amounts of light are appropriate
- Invest in low-energy bulbs; compact fluorescent bulbs, for instance, last about 8,000 hours each as opposed to 1,000 hours of the regular type. The Worldwatch Institute calculates that every compact fluorescent bulb you use saves 180 kg of coal and keeps 130 kg of carbon out of the atmosphere
- Use tungsten-halogen bulbs; they last twice as long as regular filament bulbs
- Use a timer for security lighting, adjusting weekly as the daylight changes, or choose an automatic system, triggered when someone approaches. Timers will also control room heaters, water heaters, and boilers.

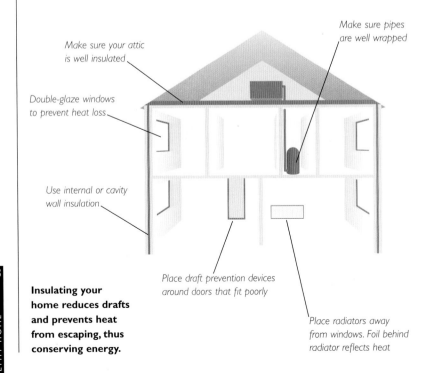

Make sure your attic is well insulated

Make sure pipes are well wrapped

Double-glaze windows to prevent heat loss

Use internal or cavity wall insulation

Place draft prevention devices around doors that fit poorly

Place radiators away from windows. Foil behind radiator reflects heat

Insulating your home reduces drafts and prevents heat from escaping, thus conserving energy.

doors and windows, using a metallic strip rather than adhesive foam, which disintegrates. You can also place draft prevention devices against the bottom of the doors. The traditional late-19th-century draft prevention device—a door curtain made from heavy chenille drape mounted on a special *portiere* rod—is also worth considering for living room doors.

Insulate or draft-proof floors, without structural work, by using thick underfelt under carpets to reduce heat loss on ground or basement levels. Put foil or a thick underlayer under linoleum or other semipermanent flooring.

Windows are one of the main sources of heat loss. Double-glazing is a highly effective form of insulation, but a layered treatment can also be used. For the layered approach, fit shutters or insulating blinds close to the glass, then add full-length lined drapes. Leave the drapes open during the day to let the sun's rays in, and close them as it begins to get dark.

Let as much sun into the house as possible; the more natural warmth and light you achieve, the less energy you will use.

Improve your heating systems by the use of a heat exchanger, also called a heat recovery ventilator (HRV). This ventilates and retains some of the heat from warm air as it leaves the house, passing it to the fresh air coming in.

SAVING WATER Thousands
of gallons of water are washed and flushed away from every home daily, particularly in places like the

United States and Europe, where householders tend to use water in a wasteful fashion. Water is a valuable resource; it needs conserving just as much as energy.

Make sure that all your faucets and pipes are tight-fitting and do not leak or drip. Install a shower with a low-flow shower head. Use the shower in preference to the bath unless you need to take a long soak. You and your partner might also want to save water by taking two baths using the same water, or reusing the water for your children's bath.

Reduce the amount of water you flush away down the toilet by installing a low-water-use cistern or by putting a brick or a marble-filled plastic container into the cistern. Make sure these do not interfere with any moving parts. Traditional suspended cisterns with a pull chain use less water than the low-level flush type, and you may want to consider installing one of these.

Get into the habit of turning off all faucets. Don't run water while you brush your teeth, shave, or wash. In the kitchen, clean vegetables and other food in a bowl of water and a colander rather than under a running faucet. Then use the water on your plants. If you wash dishes by hand, use a small bowl of hot, soapy water, and a second, larger bowl with clean, hot water for rinsing.

Think carefully about how you use water outside. Install a rain-

barrel in the garden to collect rainwater for lawns, plants, and vegetables. The softer water can also be used for hairwashing. Recycle your bath and other household water and use it for plants—be sure you have used biodegradable, nontoxic soaps and cleaners. Sprinkler systems and hoses should be avoided. Watering cans are harder work but preferable. If you do use a hose, control the flow of water carefully and use it only for your most vulnerable plants. You can conserve moisture by mulching vegetables and flowerbeds. Water the garden in the early morning or evening so water does not evaporate too quickly.

As a long-term plan, you could replace part of your lawn by a patio, and plant water-conserving ground-creeper plants, shrubs, and trees. Use shrubs, hedges, and creeper- or vine-covered trellises to shade hot, dry areas from the sun. Choose hardy house plants that need little watering.

Save water by rinsing vegetables in a bowl rather than under a running faucet.

INTRODUCING RENEWABLE SOURCES OF ENERGY

Solar panels trap heat from the sun, which can be stored and distributed through the home for washing and heating. Panels such as these are effective even on cloudy days.

MOST HOMES TODAY are still connected to main utilities, but there is an increasing move toward using alternative, or renewable, energy resources, namely sun, wind, and water, and much research is going into making these more practical for home use. Installing renewable energy systems will involve an initial financial outlay but in the long run they can not only reduce your heating and other energy costs dramatically but they can also make your home more self-sufficient and environmentally friendly.

The practicality of installing renewable systems does to some extent depend on where your property is situated, although solar panels will work almost anywhere, even in a grimy city, provided they are correctly positioned. You will require a certain amount of space for wind power machinery, a source of water if you want to sink a well or harness water power.

SOLAR energy makes maximum use of the heat from the sun. In order to harness solar power to warm your home or heat your water, you will need some specialized equipment and advice from an expert to make sure you site any solar heat exchanger or thermal storage device correctly.

There are two types of solar heating: passive and active. In passive systems, the warmth of the sun is used to warm the interior of the house. The building is specifically designed to store heat and release it at night or on cold and cloudy days; thermal storage heaters work on the same principal. Fans may be necessary to circulate the heat. Passive solar systems are relatively inexpensive to install, especially if you are restructuring your home or building a new one, and maintenance is minimal because there are no complicated structures or mechanical parts to break down. However, they are rarely adequate for all heating needs and may have to be backed up with more conventional forms of energy.

Wind is a clean, safe source of power and has been used for centuries. As yet, its domestic use is limited because of cost and concern about the visual impact of wind farms.

Active systems use solar panels, made from glass- or plastic-covered metal collector panels, sited on a sloping sun-facing roof, which absorb the heat from the sun, even on cloudy days, and store it in various ways for heating water or for whole-house heating. Because ducts, pipes, fans, pumps, and valves are necessary to distribute heat, maintenance and servicing are required. However, some systems work on the principle that hot water rises—just as hot air does—so it can circulate through the system without being pumped. Again, this type of heating is usually backed up by more conventional systems, especially in areas and at times when the hours of sunlight are short.

When you are planning the use of solar energy, remember the summer! You will be able to make maximum use of the longer hours of sunshine to heat water and for thermal storage for the cooler evenings and days, but it is essential that you consider adequate ventilation and cooling to avoid overheating. It may be necessary to incorporate shading techniques, and to have special self-opening vents that work on a temperature- or light-sensitive control.

Solar systems can also be used in greenhouses and sunrooms, both for plant growth and for trapping some extra heat for the home.

WIND AND WATER POWER

are also unlimited providers of energy and have been used for centuries—via wind-mills—to harness the wind and use it to drive machinery to grind wheat and other grains for flour. Watermills have performed similar functions, but these need a fairly fast-flowing stream.

Both wind-and water-powered generators can be used to provide domestic power, although currently they are complex and expensive. The practicality of these alternatives really does depend on the location of the property. And as anybody who has watched a raging torrent tearing down a mountain-side knows, this type of awesome landscape might be perfect for providing water power, but is not likely to be the right place to erect a home, even if it were possible to buy land and obtain permission to build on it.

Another point to keep in mind when thinking of using water as a source of energy is global warming. More and more streams and rivers are drying to a trickle, and as really cold winters become less frequent, there will be fewer mountain torrents resulting from melted snow. The water in the sea can also be used to drive turbines and generators, but this may never be practical for the single user.

Wind power is dependent on the speed and the frequency of the wind. Desert- and sea-facing sites or rounded hilltops are often the most successful position for the modern version of the windmill—the wind generator, which still relies on traditional sails to power it. In order for this to be a really feasible option, several windmills would be necessary, and research is being conducted into creating "wind farms" to harvest the wind power and supply it to communities. One concern is the despoiling of the landscape; an army of triangular metal mills marching across a hillside can be as intrusive as pylons, and they are noisy.

American architect Frank Lloyd Wright built Falling Water in Pennsylvania in the late 1930s. It remains a remarkable example of the way the natural elements can be integrated into a dwelling.

GLOSSARY

A

ACCENT COLOR—a color added to a scheme to contrast, add interest, and give a lift; can be provided in accessories added at the end of the redecorating/furnishing process

ACCESSORIES—small items such as pictures, pillows, china and glass, bath towels, statuary, etc., added to a scheme to give it a personal touch (needs to relate to the style/function of room)

ACHROMATIC COLORS—black, white, and gray—pure neutrals devoid of hue (pure color); added to a hue to create tonal variation

ANALOGOUS COLORS—closely related colors, which create harmonious schemes; next to each other on a color wheel

ARCHITECTURAL LIGHTING—light provided by fixtures that are built into the main structure

ARCHITRAVE—frame (usually wood) around the outside of a door

B

BAUBIOLOGIE—"building biology"—the (German/Scandinavian) principle of constructing healthy working and living environments based on an understanding of the relationship between the built environment and the health of people living or working in it

BIOCLIMATE—atmospheric conditions and processes affecting plant, animal, and human biology

C

CACHE POT—a decorative container placed around a plant pot to conceal it/prevent water from dripping onto a surface

CANDELA—measurement of luminous intensity equal to the brightness of one candle (approximately 12 lumens)

CFCs—Chlorofluorocarbons—used under pressure to propel aerosols from cans and also to help cooling agents circulate in refrigerators; eventually they give up their chlorine atoms, releasing them into the environment

CHAISE LOUNGE—low couch with one raised end, used as a day bed

CHI—Chi energy, which according to Chinese philosophy, breathes life into the natural world, producing harmony, growth, and well-being—in feng shui, the circulation of this energy is essential to a healthy home

CHROMA

CHROMA—measure of the intensity or saturation of a color—a pure color is high in chroma; a grayed or blackened one is low

CORNICE/COVING—decorative or curved plasterwork/wood that covers the seam between ceiling and wall

D

DADO/DADO RAIL—lower part of a wall, divided horizontally by the rail, usually decorated in a practical way to prevent damage to the wall surface; originally called a wainscoting; dado rail originally called a chair rail

DECORATIVE LIGHTING—Light fixtures, such as lamps and pendants, chosen to enhance the style of the room—often added as an accessory

DELFT RACK—shelf placed around the perimeter of a room at molding height to display china (originally blue Delftware)

E

ELEVATION—flat plan of a wall drawn to scale showing features such as doors, windows in correct position, to scale

F

FENG SHUI—Chinese philosophy blending astrology and geomancy, based on location affecting destiny; good feng shui situates buildings/arranges interiors to be in tune with nature and the universe to bring health, happiness, and prosperity to inhabitants

FIBEROPTIC—of or pertaining to optical fibers—fine strands of pure glass surrounded by a glass cladding that bends any light rays that strike it back into the center of the fiber

FRAMING PROJECTOR—light fixture that allows the beam of light to be controlled; can also project light, shadows, color on walls

FRIEZE—narrow horizontal area of wall between the cornice, coving, or ceiling and molding

G

GEOMAGNETIC FIELD—the earth's magnetic field; a geomagnetic survey will establish the position of a property in relation to this

GROW LAMPS—lighting source designed to enhance plant growth

H

HRS/V—heat recycling system/ventilator

HUE—pure color relating to the original colors of the spectrum which can be varied in chroma by the introduction of white, gray, and black to lighten, deepen, or enrich

I

INCIDENT LIGHT—light which a color appears to reflect back that relates to its lightness or value (strength)

INDUCTIVE DIMMER—special form of dimmer that must be used if low voltage lighting is to be dimmed

IR—Infrared

K

KELVIN—scale of measurement for the color temperature of light

KINETIC LIGHTING—light provided by a moving source—candle or oil lamp flame, open fire, etc.

L

LANTERN LIGHT—architectural feature when glazing is let into a void between ceiling and wall to light an area naturally—often used to light stairwells

LIGHTNESS (also VALUE)—amount of black, gray, or white in a color which determines its tonal value

LOAD-BEARING (wall)—a supporting wall, an integral part of the main structure of a building—its removal can cause the house to topple unless the load is supported by a special beam

LOW- ALLERGY HOUSE—house where dust-creating and dust-holding materials and chemicals are kept to a minimum

LUMENS—measure of light energy flowing from any one source

M

MICROCLIMATE—a special individual climate —often found in terrariums, bottle gardens, etc.— that exists separately/is different from the surrounding area

MICROWAVE—electromagnetic radiation used for fast cooking by energy absorption

N

NEUTRAL COLORS—achromatic (colorless) colors—black, white, and gray are *True* neutrals; *Accepted* neutrals are creams, beiges, off-whites— often the colors of natural and undyed materials

P

PHOTOSYNTHESIS—process by which the energy of sunlight is trapped by chlorophyll in green plants and used to build up complex materials from carbon dioxide and water

POLYURETHANE—clear varnish/sealant derivative of plastic

PVC—Polyvinylchloride, used to create many plastic products and surfaces

R

R-VALUE—measure of material's resistance to heat loss or gain—the higher the R-value, the greater the insulation capacity

RADON—a radioactive gas produced in the earth during the decaying process—can be present in many materials including granite

REFLECTIVE VALUE—the return of light waves from a surface differs, depending on its color or texture, creating high, mid, or low reflectance value—pale blues, yellows, yellow-greens have high reflective value; dark reds, blues, and purples have low

RESILIENT FLOORING—the name given to semipermanent flooring, such as linoleum, cork, rubber, that is laid over the subfloor; usually flexible, washable, and wear resistant

S

SAD—Seasonally Affective Disorder—illness and depression brought about by lack of light during winter months—can be controlled by special SAD light sources

SATURATION—the strength or vividness of a hue (color)—high saturation indicates a pure color; low saturation is a grayed/muted one

SHADE—a pure color mixed with black to deepen and enrich. In common usage, a color differing slightly from a specified hue

SOLAR ENERGY—natural energy from the sun that can be trapped and used for heating, water heating, etc.

STRUCTURAL LIGHTING—light fixtures built into the main structure of a building (architectural lighting)

T

TASK LIGHTING—lighting used specifically to illuminate a work surface or area in order for tasks to be performed

TINT—a color (hue) to which a large amount of white has been added to create a very pale value (sometimes termed a pastel color), e.g., a "tinted" white

TONAL CONTRAST—different values of color used in a scheme to provide essential contrast and visual interest

TONAL VALUE—the gradations of one color from light to dark, which is created by mixing white (to lighten); gray (to create a middle tone) and black (to darken)

TONE—a color (hue) to which a large amount of gray

TOXOCARA CANIS—a roundworm transmitted in dog feces that can cause illness and eye damage, particularly in children; lawns and earth which have been used by dogs as a toilet can remain contaminated for several years

TREATMENT—the finish on a surface, such as a wall, floor, surface, window, etc.

U

UPLIGHTERS—light fixtures designed to throw light upward—can be wall- or floor-mounted or floor-standing

UV—ultraviolet (light)

V

VALUE—the lightness or darkenss of a color or tone—its strength or weight. Changes of value are created by adding white, gray, or black to the pure color

VDT—visual display terminal, e.g., the screen of a computer or television set

VOLTAGE—LOW VOLTAGE LIGHTING— a type of lighting where a transformer is necessary to reduce the mains voltage usually to 12 volts; the transformer can be an integral part of the fixture or a separate unit installed between the main source and fixture

W

WALLWASHERS—light fixtures, usually ceiling-mounted, designed to gently wash the walls of a room with light

Y

YIN AND YANG—polar energies which in Chinese philosophy are seen as yin, passive and dark (feminine), and yang, active, and bright (masculine)

There are many organizations and retail outlets specializing in environmentally friendly products or in providing advice on ways of achieving a healthy home. The following pages list a selection of resources for the informed consumer.

Eco-building and design/energy: conservation and renewable sources of energy

American Council for an Energy-Efficient Economy
1001 Connecticut Avenue, NW
Suite 801
Washington, D.C. 20036
(202) 429-8873
Call for research and conference reports on subjects such as improving existing housing efficiency, home energy savings, and energy efficiency in building.

GoodCents
(800) 653-3445
A resource for builders, contractors, architects, and designers, who can contact GoodCents for important information on energy-efficient building and design solutions.

Holistic Options for Planet Earth Sustainability (HOPES)
University of Oregon
School of Architecture
and Allied Arts
Room 272
Lawrence Hall
Eugene, OR 97403-5249
(541) 346-0719
Resource center for architects, planners, designers, and home builders who share a concern for the health of the earth.

Energy Efficient Building Association, Inc.
2950 Metro Drive
Suite 108
Minneapolis, MN 55425
(612) 851-9940
(612) 851-9507 (fax)

The Solar Energy Network
P. O. Box 61507
Jacksonville, FL 32236-1507
(904) 786-1775 (fax)
solarinfor@solarenergy.com
General resource for solar energy information, referrals, and advice.

American Solar Energy Society
2400 Central Avenue, G-1
Boulder, CO 80301
(303) 443-3130
(303) 443-3212 (fax)
Publishes SOLAR TODAY magazine, provides up-to-date information, resources, tips about solar energy, and other renewable sources of energy.

Recycling

National Recycling Coalition
1727 King Street
Suite 105
Alexandria, VA 22514

Global Recycling Network, Inc.
2715A Montauk Highway
Brookhaven, NY 11719
(516) 286-5580
(516) 286-5551 (fax)
http://www.grn.com
Their website offers numerous links to other internet sites that deal with recycling issues and other environment topics.

Internet Consumer Recycling Guide
www.obviously.com/recycle

U.S. Environmental Hotline
800 Cleanup
Provides comprehensive information about recycling, organized by state and Zip code.
http://www.1800cleanup.org

Environmental/conservation

U. S. Environmental Protection Agency (EPA)
Public Information Center
401 M Streeet, SW
Washington, DC 20460
(202) 260-6257
Federal agency that regulates air quality, pesticide use, radon, drinking water quality, and other topics.
Call to register a complaint, or for information.

EPA Hotline
(800) 535-0202
Provides information on Resource Conservation and Recovery Act (RCRA), including the Underground Storage Tank program, Superfund programs, the Oil Pollution Act, the Emergency Planning and Community Right-to-Know Act (EPCRA); Section 112(r) of the Clean Air Act, and Spill Prevention, Control, and Countermeasure (SPCC) regulations.
http://www.epa.gov/epaoswer/hotline

Center for Health, Environment, and Justice
P. O. Box 6806
Falls Church, VA 22040
(703) 237-2249
Advises homeowners and communities on issues of environmental health.

Consumer Product Safety
Commission (CPSC)
5401 Westbard Avenue
Bethesda, MD 20207
(800) 638-2772
(800) 638-8270 (for the hearing-
impaired)
Federal agency that accepts
complaints about unsafe products
and provides legal information and
consumer tips.

Food and Drug Administration
(FDA)
Consumer Complaints Division
5600 Fishers Lane
Rockville, MD 20857
(301) 443-1240
Federal agency that answers
questions and protects consumers
against impure and unsafe foods,
drugs, and cosmetics. Call or write
to register a complaint or inquire
about a specific product.

Water

EPA Safe Drinking Water Hotline
(800) 426-4791
Provides information about laws,
regulations, and guidelines
concerning drinking water.

Water Quality Association
4151 Naperville Road
Lisle, IL 60532
(630) 505-0160
Provides information about water
quality and about technologies
available to the consumer.

National Testing Laboratories
6555 Wilson Mills Road
Cleveland, OH 44143
(800) 458-3330
Offers a complete line of
affordable water-testing kits.

Suburban Water Testing
Laboratories
4600 Kutztown Road
Temple, PA 19560
(800) 433-6595
Offers a complete line of water
testing services. Will ship a kit with
instructions for you to test your
water for lead, bacteria, metal,
minerals, industrial solvents, and
pesticides.

Allergies and asthma

American Academy of Allergy,
Asthma and Immunology
611 East Wells Street
Milwaukee, WI 53202-3889
Asthma Information and Referral
Line: (800) 822-2762
Provides written materials on
asthma, allergies, and eliminating
house dusts and allergenic irritants.

Asthma and Allergy
Foundation of America
(800) 727-8462
Provides general information and
publications as well as advice on
asthma and allergy management.

National Institute of Allergy and
Infectious Diseases
Department of Health and
Human Services
Building 31, Room 7A-50
9000 Rockville Pike
Bethesda, MD 20892
(301) 496-5717
Provides information on topics such
as pollen allergy, dust allergy, and
asthma.

**The following are mail-order
companies with national
distribution.**

Ethical consumer goods

Good Eats
P.O. Box 756
Richboro, PA 18954
(800) 490-0044
(215) 443-7087 (fax)

Harmony Seventh Generation
360 Interlocken Blvd.
Suite 300
Broomfield, CO 80021
(800) 655-3115

Nigra Enterprises
5699 Kannan Road
Agoura, CA 91301
(818) 889-6877

The Simple Living Network, Inc.
P.O. Box 233
Trout Lake, WA 98650
(800) 318-5725
(509) 395-2128 (fax)
www.slnet.com

Home and garden pesticides

National Organic Products
International, Inc.
P.O. Box 925
Mount Dora, FL 32757
(352) 383-8252
(352) 383-7307 (fax)

Bioscape
4381 Bodega Avenue
Petaluma, CA 94952
(707) 781-9233
(707) 781-9234 (fax)

Peaceful Valley Farm Supply
P.O. Box 2209
Grass Valley, CA 95945
(530) 272-4769

Planet Natural
(800) 289-6656

Natural paints, varnishes, stains

Eco-Design: The Natural Choice
1365 Rufina Circle
Santa Fe, NM 87505
(505) 438-3448
(505) 438-0199

Miller Paint Company, Inc.
12730 NE Whitaker Way
Portland, OR 97230
(503) 255-0190

Pace Chem Industries
779 La Grange Avenue
Newbury Park, CA 91320
(805) 499-2911

Natural flooring/carpeting

Carousel Carpets
1 Carousel Lane
Ukiah, CA 95482
(707) 485-0333
Call for local reps.

Desso Carpets
P.O. Box 1351
Wayne, PA 19087
(800) 368-1515
Call for local reps.

Helios Carpet
P.O. Box 1928
Calhoun, GA 30703
(800) 843-5138

Hendrickson Naturlick
P.O. Box 1677
Sebastopol, CA 95473
(707) 824-0914

Household cleaners

Auro Organics
Auro/Sinan
P.O. Box 857
Davis, CA 95617-0857
(530) 753-3104

Cal Ben Soap Company
9828 Pearmain Street
Oakland, CA 94603
(510) 638-7091

Naturally Yours
1405-C North Nias
Springfield, MO 65802
(417) 865-6260
(417) 889-3995

Simmons Pure Soaps
Simmons Handcrafts
42295 Highway 36
Bridgeville, CA 95526
(707) 777-1920

Dasun/Nonscents
P.O. Box 1677
Escondido, CA 92033
(800) 433-8929

Natural Chemistry, Inc.
244 Elm Street
New Canaan, CT 06840
(800) 753-1233

Mia Rose Products, Inc.
177-F Riverside Avenue
Newport Beach, CA 92663
(800) 292-6339

Organic foods

Garden Spot Distributors
438 White Oak Road
Box 729A
New Holland, PA 17557
(717) 354-4936
(717) 354-4934 (fax)
gardenspot@networking.com
Organically grown nuts, dried fruits,
seeds, and beans.

Gold Mine Natural Food Company
3419 Hancock Street
San Diego, CA 92110
(619) 296-8536
(619) 234-9749 (fax)
Organic grains, macrobiotic, and
healthy products for your home.

Nokomis Farm, Inc.
W2463 County Road, E.S.
East Troy, WI 53120
(414) 642-9665
(414) 642-5117 (fax)
Organic groceries, grains, and bakery
products.

Berkshire Mountain Bakery
P.O. Box 785
Housatonic, MA 01236
(802) 563-2224
Organic breads.

Woodrings Organic Food
P.O. Box 627
Milesburg, PA 16853
(814) 355-9850
Grocery products, nuts, and seeds.

Under the Sun Natural Foods
1075 Winchester Road
P.O. Box 77
Shady Valley, TN 37688
(423) 739-9266
Nuts, seeds, grains, and vitamins.

Walnut Acres Organic Farms
Penns Creek, PA 17862
(800) 433-3998
www.walnutacres.com
Produce, grains, and grocery
products.

American Health and Nutrition
508 Waymarket Drive
Ann Arbor, MI 48103
(313) 994-1897
Grains, sprouts, seeds, nuts, and
beans.

Organic gardening

Organic Food Production
Association of North America
(OFPANA)
P.O. Box 31
Belchertown, MA 01007
(413) 774-7511

Organic Growers and Buyers
Association
1405 Silver Lake
New Brighton, NM 55112
(612) 636-7933

Organic Crop Improvement
Association (OCIA)
Agrisystems
125 West Seventh Street
Wind Gap, PA 18091
(215) 863-6700

Exotic Plants
1801 Howe Avenue
Sacramento, CA 95825
(916) 922-4769
(916) 922-2351 (fax)

*Organic and hormone-free
meat and poultry*

Rising Sun Organic Food
105 Neff Road
Howard, PA 16841
(814) 355-9850

Roseland Farms
27427 M-60 West
Cassopolis, MI 49031
(616) 445-8769
(616) 445 9897 (fax)

Van Wie Natural Foods
6798 Route 9
Hudson, NY 12434
(518) 828-0533

Organic baby foods

Earth's Best
P.O. Box 887
Middlebury, VT 05753
(800) 442-4221

General resources online

Following are some websites useful
to the environmentally conscious
consumer.

Nature Conservancy
http://www.tnc.org

Sierra Club
http://www.sierraclub.org

American Council for an Energy-
efficient Economy
http://www.crest.org/aceee

Environmental Defense Fund
http://www.edf.org

Keep America Beautiful
http://www.kab.org

Solid Waste Clearinghouse
http://www.swana.org

National Wildlife Federation
http://www.nwf.org./nwf/home.html

EnviroSense
http://www.epa.gov/envirosense/
index/html

Rainforest Action Network
http://www.ran.org.

INDEX

A

accent lighting 65
accents 18, 88–9, 102–3
accidents 166
aquariums 61, 133, 138, 152–3
aerosols 127, 164
air conditioning 125, 186
air quality 113, 124–31, 134, 160, 186
allergies
    cleaning materials 174
    garden plants 148–9
    pets 151
    pollution 63, 124, 127
    soft furnishings 48, 165
alternative energy 7, 9, 180–1, 184
alternative therapies 90–1, 151
ambient lighting 65
animals 133, 150–5, 173
appetite 94
architectural lighting 64
aromatherapy 125, 127
artificial lighting 57, 64–75
asbestos 160, 161
asthma 125, 148, 151, 161, 186
attic 8, 27, 34, 178

B

background lighting 65, 66
balconies 117, 137
basements 58, 134, 141, 160
bathrooms
    cleaning materials 174, 175
    color 100, 106
    lighting 73
    planning 46–7
    water saving 179
beams 111, 168, 169, 171
bedrooms
    children 35, 50–1
    lighting 73
    planning 48–9
    sensuous 130–1
beds
    bedding 165
    four-poster 116–17
    mattress 165, 167

storage space 34
bells 119
birdcages 139, 151
birds 119, 154
black 99, 107
bleach 174–5
blinds 60–1, 62, 88
blood pressure 92
blue 78, 80, 85, 92, 104, 107
breathing 127
bricks 61, 87, 109–10, 125

C

calm 18
color 90, 92, 104, 106
    Feng Shui garden 147
    fish 152
    pattern 109
    water features 123, 147
candles 63, 73, 74, 75, 128, 131
carpets
    allergies 185, 186
    noise 117
    pattern 109
    pollutants 163
    safety 166
cats 133, 150–2
ceiling racks 34
ceilings, low 141, 168
cellars 34
chandeliers 64, 66
chemicals 79, 161, 162, 164, 174
chi 14, 123, 135, 140, 153, 168
children
    bedrooms 50–1
    design considerations
    16–17, 26
    pets 150
    safety 166
cleaning materials 127, 128, 161, 164–6,
    174–5, 186
clocks 119
closets 34, 37, 49, 50
clutter 15, 34–7, 49, 166, 168
colds 124, 125

color 77–111
contrast 100–3
    increasing light 58
    increasing space 92
    and light 81, 84–5
    matching 105
    perceiving 84–5
    planning 17–18, 100–3
    plants 140–1, 144, 146
    psychology 92–103
    temperature 71
    and texture 86–9
    therapy 90–1
    wheel 80–1, 100–7
complementary colors 102, 103
compost 147, 148, 151, 173
computers 52–3, 71, 134, 141, 186
concealed lighting 64, 67
condensation 125
conservation 9, 176, 184, 185
cool colors 81, 92–3, 98, 104
corners 166, 168
crystals 62, 63
cupboards 34, 35, 37
curtains 60, 109, 116, 127
cushions and pillows 88–9, 108

D

daylight bulbs 69, 168
decorating
    preparations 27
    safety 166
decorative lighting 64
desk lamps 65, 67
dining rooms 40–1, 72–3
display lighting 65
dogs 133, 150–1, 152
downlighters 64, 67, 69
drafts 39, 116, 117, 178–9
dust mites 160, 161
dyes 78–9

E

earth, Feng Shui 14, 82
eco-design 9, 170–3, 184

electricity
  alternative energy 180–1
  appliances 63, 125, 160, 176–7
  conserving 176–7
  radiation 63, 141, 160
  safety 63, 64, 166
energy
  alternative 180–1, 184
  conserving 9, 176–7, 178–9, 184
  Feng Shui 14, 63, 82, 123, 140, 153, 168
entrances 38–9, 74, 135, 141, 168
environmentally friendly homes 7, 9, 157–81, 184, 185–6
essential oils 127, 128
ethical consumer advice 186, 187
exhaust fans 125, 128
exhaust hoods 45, 125
external decoration 25, 110–11
eye irritation 161

F

fabric
  dyes 78–9
  flame-retardant 165
  noise control 116–17
  pollutants 163, 165
  recycling 172
  texture 87
Feng Shui 14–15
  bathrooms 46–7
  bedrooms 49, 51, 73
  color 82–3, 90
  dining rooms 41
  entrances 39, 135
  fish 153
  gardens 147
  halls 39
  healing measures 90, 168–9
  kitchens 45
  light 62–3, 66, 75
  living rooms 43
  new homes 21–2
  plants 140–1, 168

sound 118
space and harmony 28–9, 33
sunrooms 54
workrooms 52–3
fire
Feng Shui 14, 82
  light 63, 67, 71, 131
  pollution 161
  safety 42, 166, 167
fish 61, 133, 138, 152–3
Five Elements 14–15, 82
floor plan 30
flooring
  cleaning materials 175
  energy conservation 179
  materials 114, 117, 185, 186
  pattern 108, 109
  pollution 161, 162–3
  safety 166
flowers 127, 128, 136,140, 154
fluorescent light 64, 67, 69
formaldehyde 18, 125, 160, 161
full-spectrum lighting 69
furniture
  placement 27, 32–3, 34
  polish 164–5, 175
  pollution 161, 164–5
  recycling 171–2, 173
  safety 166
  shape 33

G

games rooms, lighting 73
garden
  Feng Shui 147
  lighting 74–5
  low allergen 148–9
  orientation 21
  planning 13
  plants 132, 144–7
  shed 35, 74, 167
  water saving 179
  wildlife 154–5
glass
  bricks 61

chandeliers 66
increasing light 59
insulation 54, 116, 178, 179
recycling 172, 173
shelves 36, 132, 137
glossary 182
gray 99, 107
green 80, 98, 104
greenhouses 137, 142–3, 162
gyms 53

H

halls 38–9, 72, 141, 168
hanging baskets 34, 137, 146
harmony
  color schemes 51, 92, 98, 101
  Feng Shui 14–15
  neighbors 117
  planning space 24–55
hay fever 148
headaches 49, 124, 161
healthy home
  creating 12–15
  definition 10–11
  heating 176, 178, 179, 180–1
herbs
  growing 113, 137, 138, 144, 154
  low-allergen gardens 148, 149
  scents 128, 129
hooks 34–5, 37
house plants 133, 134–7, 179
humidity 113, 125, 128, 134
hygiene 99, 152, 174

I

incandescent light 69
indirect lighting 64, 67
insomnia 92
insulation 20
  energy conservation 176, 178–9
  noise 114, 121
pollution 160, 161
interior design 8–9, 10, 13
Internet sites 187
ionizers 113, 125, 186

K

kitchen
cleaning materials 174–5
energy conservation 176, 177
lighting 73
pattern 109
planning 34, 44–5
plants 168
recycling 173
safety 166
smells 127
water saving 179

L

ladders 167
lamps 64, 67
landings, lighting 72
laundry 174, 176
lead 160, 161
life style 16–19
light
artificial 57, 64–75
and color 80, 84–5, 87
electrical safety 64, 166
energy conservation 178
Feng Shui 62–3, 168
fixtures 64–7
levels 71
lighting plan 65
natural 57, 58–63, 179
planning 18, 70–1
sources 68–9
linoleum 163
living room 42–3, 72
living things 132–55
low-voltage lighting 69, 74

M

mattresses 165, 167
measuring 30
metal
cleaner 175
Feng Shui 14, 82, 119
recycling 172, 173
mirrors 39, 61, 63, 131, 132, 168
monochromatic schemes 101, 106

mood 57, 65, 77, 80, 104–7
moonlight 63
multifunctional rooms 27, 40, 50, 53, 72
music 113, 114, 120–1

N

natural light 57, 58–63, 173, 179
natural products
benefits 18–19
building materials 110–11
cleaning 128
color 107
fabrics 113, 163, 165
floorings 163, 186
texture 87
nature
links 18, 55, 98, 132, 142–7
sounds of 118, 119
neighbors 117, 120, 122, 152
neutral colors 81, 96, 99, 104, 107
new homes
choosing 20–1
geomagnetic survey 160
living with 12–13
pollutants 160–1
noise 18, 114–17, 121, 122, 187

O

oil lamps 68, 73, 74, 75
orange 80, 96
ornaments 88, 173

P

paint
increasing light 58
lead 79, 160, 161, 164
pigments 78–9
pollutants 161, 162, 164, 165
safety 166
texture 87
paper, recycling 172–3
patio 13, 21, 132, 138
pattern 104, 108–9
pendant light 65, 66
pets 132, 150–2

pictures 88, 108, 131
pigments 78–9
pink 95
planning 13, 16–17, 26–7
plans
floor and wall 30–1
lighting 65
plants 132–49
air quality 52, 125, 134
Feng Shui 140–1, 168
house 133, 134–7, 179
lighting 74–5, 131, 132, 141
low allergen 148–9
sounds 119
sunrooms 54
plastics 160, 161, 173
playrooms 27, 73, 106
polish 164–5, 175
pollution 9, 11, 18, 125, 134, 160–5
pomander 129
ponds 123
porch 117, 178
posture 127
potpourri 128, 129
primary colors 80, 103
purple 78, 80, 93, 104

R

radiation 125, 141, 160, 168
recycling 7, 13
building materials 162, 170–1, 173
compost 147, 148, 151, 173
furniture 171–2
plant containers 138–9
textiles 172
waste 172–3
red 38, 80, 85, 95, 169
relaxation 106–7, 113, 122–3
renewable energy 180
reptiles 133
rugs 88, 109, 117, 166, 172

S

SAD see seasonal affective disorder
safety 42, 45, 63, 64, 73, 166–7

salvage 13, 27, 170–1, 185

scents 18, 112, 126–31

seasonal affective disorder (SAD) 57, 69, 186

secondary colors 80, 103

security 75, 121, 166, 178

sensuality 18, 113, 130, 144

shelves 19, 34, 37

   glass 36, 132, 137

   safety 166

shiny surfaces 87, 88, 89, 106, 168

showers 46

sick building syndrome 125

skylights 61

smells 126–7

smoking 128, 160, 161

soft furnishings, pollutants 163

solar energy 20, 143, 180–1

sound 112, 113–21

space

   planning 24–55

   using color 92, 93, 98, 104

   using pattern 108

spotlights 64, 67

stairs

   cupboards 35

   lighting 72

   safety 166

standard lamps 65, 67

stimulating

   colors 94, 96, 97, 106

   patterns 108, 109

storage 34–7

stress

   color blue 92

   pets 132, 150

   plants 136

   sound 113, 115, 118

structural lighting 64

sunlight 58, 62

sunrooms

   insulation 178

   light 61, 74

   planning 13, 54–5

   plants 132, 137, 138, 142–3

   water 122

swimming pools 122, 123

synthetic materials 128

T

table lamps 65, 67

task lighting 65, 67

television 43, 71, 73

terrariums 139

tertiary colors 80

texture 86–9, 106, 113, 130

thrift 7, 13

tiles 87, 108, 109, 168, 173

toilets 46–7, 179

touch 113, 130, 144

tungsten halogen lamps 69, 178

tungsten lighting 69

U

upholstery 42, 163, 165

uplighters 64, 69

V

varnish 162, 164, 166, 186

vegetables 146

ventilation 124–5, 128, 160

vinyl 18, 162, 165

violet 80, 93

W

wall coverings 79, 163–4, 171

wall hangings 88, 172

wall lights 65, 67

wall plan 30

walls 34, 109

wallwashers 64, 67, 69, 72

warm colors 81, 94, 97, 98, 105

washing 174, 176

waste, recycling 173, 185

water

   conservation 9, 20, 179

   energy conservation 176, 178

   Feng Shui 14, 82, 123, 147

   heating 180–1

   lead pipes 161

   low-allergen gardens 148

   power 181

   relaxation 113, 122–3

   safety 166

   sound 18, 118

white 12, 99, 104, 107

wildlife 123, 146, 154–5

wind chimes 39, 119

wind power 181

windows

   insulation 20, 178, 179

   natural light 59–61

   plants 132, 136–7

   safety 166

   ventilation 124, 160

wood

   Feng Shui 14, 82

   recycling 171–2

   sustainability 165

   texture 87

   treatments 161, 162

   wind chimes 119

workrooms 27, 52–3, 73

Y

yellow 80, 85, 97

ACKNOWLEDGMENTS

The publishers would like to thank the following for the use of pictures:

Abode Interiors Photography & Library: pp 16, 17(b), 28(br), 33(ab), 34(ab), 35, 40(t), 42(t), 42(m), 46(bl), 48(m), 50/51, 51, 60(t), 64, 66(tl), 66(ml), 66/67, 67(b), 71, 80(bl), 80/81, 94/95, 96(bl), 99(tl), 101(t), 101(b), 102(t), 103(t), 104, 105(t), 106(bl), 107(bl), 116(t), 118(tr), 136(t)

AKG London: p 68(t)

Arcaid/Richard Bryant: pp 8, 13
Arcaid/Scott Frances: p181
Arcaid/Steve Lyman: p 111(tr)
Arcaid/Alberto Piovano: p 9(ab)
Arcaid/Petrina Tinslay/Belle: p12
Arcaid/Richard Waite: p 8
Arcaid/Rodney Weidland/Belle: pp 11(b),171(t)

Concord Lighting Limited: p 69

John Cullen Lighting: p 75(bl)

Creation Baumann: p 109(t)

Elizabeth Whiting Associates: pp18, 19, 20(m), 20(b), 21, 24/25, 28(tl), 33(m), 34(b), 38(tl), 38(ml), 38(bl), 38(br), 40(m), 44, 46/47, 47, 48(b), 54/55, 55, 56/57, 58, 59, 60(bl)(br), 61(bl), 66(bl), 67(t), 76/77, 79(mr), 86(ml), 89(tr), 93, 97, 98(b), 95(br), 99(mr), 102(b) 111(tl), 112/113, 116(m),116(b), 122, 123(l), 124(tl), 132/133, 136(b), 137(t), 143(m)(br), 145(b) 150(t), 168, 170, 171(b), 172(b),180

Garden Picture Library: pp 9(b), 118(bl), 119(tr), 123(r), 138(t)(m)(b), 139(t)(m), 143(tl), 144(tl)(bl), 144/145, 146, 147(br), 149, 150(b), 154(t)(m)(b), 155, 158/9, 179

Walter Gardiner Photography: p 28

Gleneagles: p 90(br)

Harlequin fabrics & wallcoverings: p 109(b)

Heron Parigi: p 52

Houses & Interiors/Rodger Brooks: pp 15, 50
Houses & Interiors/Simon Butcher: pp 17(ab), 38(ml), 108(r), 126(bl)
Houses & Interiors/Mark Bolton: pp 46(br), 61(br), 124(b)
Houses & Interiors/Gwenan Murphy: p 139(bl)

The Hutchison Library: p 115,181

The Image Bank: pp 20(tl), 45, 48(t), 78(ml), 80(tl), 82(tr), (mr),(b)(bl), 83,84(t),(b), 84/85, 91(bl), 96(tl)(tr), 108(l), 110(t), 110(b), 111(bl), 114/115, 120, 151, 152, 152/153, 153(m)(br)

Laura Ashley: pp 92(l), 107(t)

Netsurfer Ltd: p 53

Courtesy of Pioneer: p 121

The Stock Market Photo Agency: pp 6/7, 11(ab),14, 21, 90(l), 96/97, 98(tr), 99(br)

The publishers would like to thank the following for help with photography:

C & H Fabrics Ltd, Brighton; Luggage Plus, Lewes; Robert Hoare
(Pine Antiques), Lewes